# MY SON MARSHALL, MY SON EMINEM

# MY SON MARSHALL, MY SON EMINEM

## Setting the record straight
### on my life as Eminem's mother

## DEBBIE NELSON
### with Annette Witheridge

JOHN BLAKE

John Blake Publishing Ltd
Published by John Blake Publishing Ltd,
3 Bramber Court, 2 Bramber Road,
London W14 9PB, UK

www.blake.co.uk

First published in hardback in 2007

ISBN: 978-1-84454-456-1

British Library Cataloguing-in-Publication Data:
A catalogue record for this book is available from the British Library.

Design by www.envydesign.co.uk

Printed in Great Britain by William Clowes Ltd, Beccles, Suffolk

1 3 5 7 9 10 8 6 4 2

Papers used by John Blake Publishing are natural, recyclable products made
from wood grown in sustainable forests. The manufacturing processes
conform to the environmental regulations of the country of origin.

This book is dedicated to the memory of my brothers, Ronald 'Ronnie' Polkingharn (1972–1991) and Todd Nelson Senior (1961–2004).

To my beloved Nan, Betty Whitaker (1912–2000).

And, last but not least, DeShaun Holton, a.k.a. Proof (1973–2006).

May they rest in peace.

# ACKNOWLEDGEMENTS

First of all I would like to thank God because with Him all things are possible.

I would also like to thank all my friends, relatives and others who I have met through my journey in life, who held me up, believed in me and were there through the trying times.

Also, my sons Marshall and Nathan. They are my world.

I would also like to thank my co-writer Annette Witheridge, my agent James Wills, John Blake Publishing, James Mann and everyone else who believes in me.

# CONTENTS

# INTRODUCTION

There was a time not so long ago when I had every-thing I ever dreamed of – two loving sons Marshall and Nathan, a great job running my own limousine business and several houses I'd turned into real homes. No one was prouder than I was when Marshall turned his talent for writing poetry into rap. I encouraged him every step of the way. It wasn't easy and Marshall was no overnight sensation. The skinny white dude, as he called himself, was often laughed off stage and mocked by the hardcore Detroit musicians and radio disc jockeys he was so desperate to impress. Along the route he ditched his first professional name M&M – a play on his initials – and became Eminem the foul-mouthed entertainer.

At first I went along with it for Marshall's sake – if I

made one mistake as a mother it was giving in to my eldest son's every whim. He never knew his father and I did all I could to make up for it. I wasn't happy when he made up a whole new life for himself – what mother wants to be known as a pill-popping alcoholic who lives on welfare? To tell the truth, I was heartbroken. The lies started coming thick and fast – and not just from Marshall. Relatives claimed I'd abandoned him as a baby; his father alleged he'd spent years trying to find us but we'd just disappeared. None of it was true but the fibs kept getting bigger, and ultimately Marshall and I became estranged. I think he's forgotten the good times we had, and this book is my way of setting the record straight.

As a child, Marshall would tear around the house in a Batman cape, jump on the sofa to battle imaginary foes, then crash exhausted onto my lap. Our home was full of music. Marshall mimed in front of the mirror. He filled notebooks with poetry and cartoon-superhero drawings. Between the ages of 11 and 13, he charged younger kids 25 cents to watch him breakdance.

He doted on his little brother Nathan, who copied everything he did. Nathan too loved Ninja Turtles and superheroes.

Marshall and I were so close that friends and relatives commented that it was as if the umbilical cord had never been cut. He confided in me throughout his teens; no subject was taboo. When he came home deflated, I told him he could achieve anything he wanted.

2

'Kim says I'm a nobody, nothing but a hamburger flipper,' he said after one especially brutal fallout with his girlfriend when he was working as a $5.50-an-hour fast-food chef.

As everyone knows, Marshall proved his critics wrong. He became the biggest star in the music world, with an Oscar, nine Grammy awards and countless MTV trophies to his name. He's a billion-dollar industry and has broken numerous sales records. With the release of the film *8 Mile* in 2002 he became the only artist ever to top the movie, album and singles chart at the same time. He is constantly compared to Elvis Presley, who a generation earlier took the music of poor black people and turned it mainstream. Marshall did the same with rap – but it came at an unimaginable price not only to him, but all of us who loved him.

After his first album, *Infinite*, flopped, he reinvented himself as white trailer trash with a crazy welfare mom. I was shocked when I first heard his lyrics – Marshall rarely swore much in front of me. But he constantly reassured me it was all a big joke.

'The more foul I am, the more they love me,' he said.

And so began the great Eminem show.

Many things have been said about my son since he rocketed to fame in 1999 with *The Slim Shady LP*. American President George W. Bush called him 'the most dangerous threat to American children since polio'. Learned professors have dissected his lyrics, and – unbelievably to me – his concerts have been likened to

3

Hitler Youth rallies because of the way he supposedly whips up anger. He's also been compared to the poets Robert Burns and Gerard Manley Hopkins. Depending on who you believe, he's a woman-hating, gay-bashing gangster or a genius with a talent for irony.

Marshall and Nathan were among the people who inspired me to write this book when they started asking me about my own childhood. They knew I'd had a difficult life and wanted to know more. I'd hidden my struggles to bring them up because I never wanted to worry them about anything. I often juggled several jobs to make sure they had everything they wanted. Then Marshall confessed that he was so strung out on drink and drugs that he could recall nothing of 1999. The hits, the concerts and even his first wedding were all a blur.

No one prepares you for the downside of celebrity. There isn't a school for would-be stars and their families, where you can learn about the pitfalls. Marshall says fame brought a slew of problems he never expected. He no longer trusts anyone. Everyone wants a piece of Eminem the megastar, not Marshall Mathers the man. I call these people the circling vultures: they spot dollar signs and swoop in for the kill.

My son never intended for me to become an object of hatred. He did not want to believe it when he discovered fans spat at me in the supermarket and stuck chewing gum in my hair. It's not just the fans. Their parents sneer at me, too, because they do not realise Marshall was reared in a loving, creative environment. I'm not saying

4

I was the perfect mother – far from it, as you will read – but I did my best.

I've been described as much maligned. Misunderstood is more accurate. Strangers assume they know me because of songs like 'Cleanin' Out My Closet (I'm Sorry Mama)', but until now only Marshall and I knew the real truth. It wasn't just the hurtful things involving drink and drugs. Everyone believed I was an evil, abusive monster. Even professionals like police officers, court officials and hospital staff treated me badly because of what they'd heard about me.

Over the following chapters I'll not only explain how I came to be tarred as a pill-popping alcoholic but will also tell the real stories behind my son's lyrics, along with the happy times and the tragedies that touched our lives. Two of my three brothers died young, violent deaths. I want to tell their stories, too. I'm a fighter and I will never give up. My beloved Nan had a wonderful old saying: 'The truth will stand when the world's on fire.' This book is all about that.

Debbie Nelson
Michigan, September 2007

# CHAPTER ONE

I was 14 going on 30 when I fell in love with Marshall Bruce Mathers Jr. I'd climbed a big old apple tree to escape my drunken stepfather when Bruce, as he was known, suddenly appeared. He squared up to my stepfather, and told him he'd regret it if he ever hit me again.

Bruce was four years older than I was – a lean six-foot-two tall with beautiful long brown hair that he wore in a ponytail. He played the drums and was crazy about The Doors. Lots of girls in St Joseph, Missouri, had the hots for him. I was a skinny little tomboy with a bad overbite, so the last thing I expected was a romance with someone as tall and strong as Bruce. But that day changed everything. He offered me something no one had offered before – protection from my family.

It didn't matter what went wrong at home, it was always my fault. That evening I didn't wash the dishes quickly enough, so Mom went for me. I managed to push her off before running out of the house and clambering up the tree.

I heard Mom scream from inside, 'Find the kid and beat her!'

My stepfather was swinging a belt around, swearing drunkenly. An apple fell to the ground. The branches around me creaked. I was terrified they'd find me. Then Bruce appeared.

'When you find her, you're not going to lay a finger on her,' I heard Bruce say. 'If you've got any weapons, throw them down. You want to fight, then hit me. We'll fight man to man.'

My stepfather tried to change the subject by asking for a cigarette. Then he scurried off back inside.

It was just going dark and I was frightened Bruce would leave, so I called down to thank him for saving me.

'What are you doing up there?' he asked, amazed I'd managed to hide myself so well.

I scrambled down the tree, jumping the last few feet into his arms.

'They're not going to put their hands on you any more,' he said. 'No one's going to hurt you again, Debbie.'

He looked deep into my eyes and all my fears disappeared. I could hardly believe it. Suddenly Bruce was the big brother I'd always wanted. And more. He was the first man in my miserable life to show he cared.

If only I'd known then how wrong I could be.

Looking back on my childhood, I find I have few fond memories. I was born in 1955 on a military base in Kansas. My parents, Bob and Betty Nelson, fought nonstop. I was the eldest and a total daddy's girl. I recall sitting with my German shepherd dog on the front porch at Nan's house in Warren, Michigan, where we lived at the time, waiting for Dad to come home from work. If I tried to stray into the road my dog would pull me back towards the house.

I also remember standing with Mom waiting for surplus food outside an old government warehouse. By the time my younger brothers, Steve and Todd, were born, I was going alone to collect canned meat, dried beans, powdered eggs and milk while Mom waited nearby in the car. It could take several hours to reach the front of the food queue. Sometimes the men who worked there helped me carry the heavy cardboard boxes to the car. On other occasions they yelled at me to keep moving. I hated every minute of it but it helped feed us. Aged 11, I was keeping house, caring for my brothers, cooking and cleaning.

Dad's mother, Bessie 'Betty' Whitaker, whom we all called Nan, was the only woman in my large dysfunctional family to show us kids love. She was the nearest thing I had to a real mother. I adored spending summers with her. It meant a rest from the chores, the screaming matches and violence at home. I felt secure snuggled up next to her.

Nan's house in Warren was quiet. Our homes – and we moved constantly – weren't. There was always noise. I was 7 when my parents first split up. Todd was a baby and Dad claimed he wasn't his son. Steve, who was three years younger than I was, and I stayed with Dad. I remember trying to cook breakfast and setting the frying pan on fire. I was terrified I'd burned the house down. We went home to Mom.

Dad was back with us when Mom met Ron Gilpin, the man who was to become my stepfather. Mom used me as cover when she sneaked off to see Gilpin. He'd give me his loose change and tell me not to tell Dad. Everything unravelled when my sister Tanya was born in 1964. This time Dad found himself a girlfriend and left for good.

Dad married Geri and adopted her two children. One of them was called Debbie, just like me. That broke my heart. It meant there were two Debbie Nelsons and he obviously preferred his adopted daughter to me. He turned his back on us completely, acting as though we didn't exist. Poor Nan did her best to make up for his disappearance. She tried to arrange meetings but Dad rarely showed up. And when he did, he mocked us because we were small and scrawny.

I retreated into my own little world of make-believe. I carried a picture of my father in his Air Force uniform everywhere with me and told my school friends that he was dead, that he'd been horribly maimed in a train wreck. People said Dad looked like Elvis Presley, so I

10

pretended we were related to him and the singer Ricky Nelson. Before he retired from the military we'd lived a nomadic life, spending time on bases in California, Italy and Germany. I would close my eyes and try to magic us back to Europe.

Mom married Gilpin but they split up constantly. She worked behind the bar at an exotic dance club. She attracted drunken bullies and the cycle was always the same. After the initial courtship, the drinking and fighting and leaving would start again. There were many nights when we kids slept on the outside porch with mom to escape beatings.

In fairness, Mom didn't know any better. She was just 14 when she married Dad, who was 19, and 15 when she had me to escape her horrible family. Yet, instead of giving us the happy childhood she'd never had, unknown to her she made our lives miserable. Not that it put her off having more children. In 1968, when I was 12, she was once again with Gilpin and gave birth to Betti Renee. Mom – now known as Big Betty – favoured Little Betti and didn't hide the fact. The rest of us, according to Mom and Dad, were stupid and unwanted. Is it any wonder I grew up believing I was worthless?

I ran away from home at the age of 12 after my stepfather attacked me. I was in the upstairs bathroom when he barged in, grabbed hold of me and tried to rip my clothes off. His breath reeked of alcohol; his face was twisted with lust. He loomed above me, rocking drunkenly back and forth as I screamed my head off, yelling at my brothers to call the police. Steve, who was nine, and six-year-old Todd burst into the bathroom and tried to kick him away but he was too big and strong for them. The police arrived. They took my stepfather off in handcuffs and I stupidly thought that was the last we'd see of him. But Mom refused to believe me. My stepfather returned home after a night in jail and I left. I thought he'd kill me the next time he got his hands on me.

My best friends Theresa and Bonnie provided sanctuary. Their mothers taught me about families and love. They wanted to adopt me. They made me feel like a real person. The trouble was, I missed my little brothers. Home was horrible for them too and they said it was unbearable when I wasn't there. Running away became a pattern. I'd lie low for a few days, and then Steve or Todd would beg me to return. So I'd go home, things would be fine for a week, then the fighting would start again.

School kept me sane, especially when Theresa and I joined the cheerleading squad. Her mom made our outfits and for the first time I felt cool. Bonnie was a couple of years older and introduced us to music. She played the guitar. We lived for Janis Joplin and Jimi Hendrix. We were hippie chicks and – as far as we were concerned – mature beyond our years.

Edna and Charles Schwartz lived up the road from us. They had no children, so they doted on her nephew Bruce. His family lived in North Dakota but he often visited. Bruce stayed with them and for a while he had no work. Then a few months later he got a job at the local wood-veneer factory. Bonnie had a crush on Bruce, and I trailed shyly behind her as she set about getting to know him better for me.

We spent hours in the park listening to music. Bruce said he was a drummer and talked about forming a band. He was also kind to my brothers when we met at baseball games. I felt totally at ease with him. It wasn't a sexual thing. He listened to me, gave advice and made me laugh.

Compared with every boy I knew, Bruce was sophisticated. Romantically, I thought he was way out of my league. But, after he had rescued me from my stepfather, we started talking about our hopes and dreams for the future. I told him I prayed every night for a better life than Mom's. All I ever wanted was a husband who loved me, a nice home and a big brood of children. Bruce felt the same. As we sat in the darkness discussing the future, I truly believed that all my dreams had come true.

# CHAPTER TWO

You can marry – with parental permission – at 15 in Missouri. One night, after an especially bitter fight at home, I told Bruce I was going to run away again. I couldn't stand the babysitting, my drunken stepdad and the constant battles with Mom. To my surprise, he proposed. Of course I said yes. I was in love. Initially Mom refused to give her permission.

We used to hang out at Jonas' Coffee House listening to music. I would watch adoringly as Bruce pounded pencils on the table, pretending to be a drummer. He was into heavy-metal music and he let his hair flow free as he worked his way into a drumming frenzy. He had the high cheekbones of a Blackfoot Indian and claimed the Mathers family was descended from witches.

He'd tease me, saying, 'You'd better watch out when

you go to sleep: I turn into a vampire.' Then he'd bare his teeth at me. It was only a joke but I was so frightened of violence that I used to cower. Bruce would put his big arms around me, telling me not to worry.

Bruce had two cousins, who were both lovely. They looked after me. Then there were Theresa and Bonnie and all our friends. We were a big happy crowd, whiling away hours in the local park. Someone always had a guitar, so we'd sit in a circle singing or talking until the police arrived at midnight. They'd order us to leave. As far they were concerned we were a group of no-good hippies.

Not that everything was perfect in paradise. Bruce and I disagreed when it came to sex. He wanted it immediately. I wanted to wait until we married. Even though I acted as mother to my siblings and felt I'd lived a lifetime of chores and drudgery, I had few clues about how motherhood came about.

My Catholic mom had instilled in me early on that sex was dirty. When I was almost 13 I started my periods, and she said, 'Now the guys will come round and you'll be pregnant before you know it.' She never told me about the birds and bees but Theresa helpfully filled me in, warning that if a boy even put his arm around me I could conceive. I had my first 'pregnancy scare' a few months later, when a lad called Mark tried to cuddle me at the drive-in movie theatre. I pushed him away, went home, filled a small vanity case with rocks and dropped it constantly on my stomach, hoping to miscarry.

Eventually, I told Theresa, who laughed her head off, then took me home to her mother for a proper chat.

Bruce was my first boyfriend. He was experienced but all the fumbling around frightened me. We kissed all the time but I pushed him away every time his hands slipped into my clothes. It was, perhaps, inevitable that he looked elsewhere for sex. I heard rumours that he was cheating on me but he denied it. I wanted to believe him. I wanted so much for everything to be right between us. So I closed my eyes, thought of our future together and gave him my virginity.

It still wasn't enough. A few months later I was on the phone to Bruce when the local whore came knocking at his door. She had the hots for him and didn't bother to hide it from me. I screamed at Bruce not to let her in, but he claimed they were just friends and told me not to be so jealous. I slammed the phone down and went running over to his place. She heard me shouting and ran down the back steps to escape. I told Bruce there and then I wouldn't marry him, and then I stalked off. He chased after me, grabbing hold of my arms, pleading with me to believe nothing had happened. I wanted to trust him, I really did, but my childhood insecurities about being ugly and worthless kicked in. It didn't help when he later confessed he had – just once – slept with her. He claimed it didn't mean a thing and again he got down on his knees begging me to marry him.

Mom finally agreed to give me her permission to marry. I left the consent forms with her when she was sick in hospital and didn't bother to check her signature when I collected them a few hours later. I steamed ahead with our wedding plans, not realising my aunt Martha had signed her name, pretending to be my mother.

I'd abandoned my Catholic faith – although the guilt about sex remained with me for years – around the time Mom started seeing Gilpin. She'd used church as an excuse to sneak out and see him. I tried several different denominations, even toying with the Jehovah's Witnesses for a while. By the summer of 1970 I was attending the Assembly of God Church in the basement of St Joseph's East Mills Shopping Mall. Bruce came with me just once to appease me. I decided the underground chapel was perfect for our little wedding.

We married on 20 September 1970. I wore a cream just-above-the-knee dress with a red velvet vest. Bruce splashed out on a smart tailored suit. Dad actually showed up to walk me down the aisle. Mom was there too, finally to give us her blessing. All my family and friends came, along with Bruce's dad Marshall and his mother Rae. I was the happiest bride ever – even though the whole ceremony was illegal because the signature on the consent form wasn't Mom's, although I didn't know that at the time.

We couldn't afford a honeymoon. Anyway, I was still at school and Bruce couldn't get time off from his job at the Missouri Valley Veneer wood company. It wasn't easy finding a home. Anyone with long hair was considered a layabout, so Bruce hid his ponytail under a cap.

I dropped out of school. It was stupid, really, because I was bright, often helping friends with their homework. But I was a married woman of 16. It made sense to concentrate on creating a home.

When Bruce and I celebrated our first wedding anniversary with a romantic home-cooked meal I thanked him for making me happy. My horrible childhood memories were behind me.

The only blight on the horizon was my failure to get pregnant. We couldn't wait to become parents. Every two months or so I went running off to the doctor but it wasn't to be. I was tiny – five-foot-two tall and always under 100 pounds (that's 7 stone, or 45 kilos). The doctor lectured me constantly about being too skinny. I couldn't help it. I had a big appetite but was naturally scrawny. The doctor would order me to go home, put on a bit of weight and learn to relax. He told me to be patient, and then I'd get pregnant.

Mom divorced Gilpin, married Ronald Polkingharn and was soon pregnant with her sixth child.

I suppose for Bruce it wasn't the easiest of starts to married life. His parents loved him unconditionally and he had just one elder sister, Carol Sue, who was in the military, serving in Japan. He'd never come across a family like mine.

He promised that our children would never suffer the way I had. So every night I prayed to God that I'd be with child. In January 1972 those prayers were answered. After sixteen months of marriage, I was finally pregnant.

21

# CHAPTER THREE

I loved being pregnant. I was so proud of my tiny belly and tried to make it stick out more because I wanted the world to know I was expecting a baby. I sang songs as I rubbed my stomach. 'Baby Love' and 'Love Child' by Diana Ross and the Supremes were particularly fitting. Motown Music came out of Detroit – just a few miles from Nan's house in Warren, Michigan, where I'd spent the only happy times of my childhood.

Nan was the family historian. She was proud of her Cherokee Indian heritage and had boxes of old documents and photos. Now I wanted to know everything about our ancestors so that one day I could tell my own child. Nan could track back to Betsy Webb, forced, with seventeen thousand Cherokees, from the Deep South to march west to Oklahoma during the brutal winter of 1838–9. More than four thousand died along what became known as the Trail of Tears. Nan was proud of Betsy Webb, who she said was in all the history books along with another forefather, Washington Harris. Many years later Nan's knowledge proved invaluable when I used our links with Alabama's Echota tribe for help to battle the child protection authorities – a story you will read all about later.

Mom could trace her family back to Great Britain. Her great grandmother, Ailsa Macallister, sailed from Scotland to New York, at the age of 23, in 1870. My great-granny, Martha Mount, inherited a Scottish love of whisky and terrified us kids by chasing her husband around with a fire poker. She called cabs to collect her booze. There was a constant stream of taxi drivers bearing bottles at her door.

She would get really mean with Grandpa and the other kids but favoured me because I was born on her birthday.

Bruce, who'd been born a few miles from the Canadian border in Fort Fairfield, Maine, was part Blackfoot Indian. The Mathers name originated in Scotland, although he thought his branch came from rural Wales. He'd grown up hearing stories of a book about the black arts, apparently detailing the Mathers links to witchcraft. We discovered a creepy British occultist called Samuel Liddel MacGregor Mathers, who'd founded the Order of the Golden Dawn. He was an early mentor of the hedonistic witch Aleister Crowley. Bruce loved that. He was mad about heavy-metal music, and Led Zeppelin's Jimmy Page lived in Crowley's Scottish mansion.

Now, when Bruce bared his teeth at me and pretended to be a warlock, I really was frightened. He also terrorised my brothers, who spent most of their time with us. I had no problems feeding them and helping with homework, but it really started to get to Bruce, especially when he was trying to sleep after his night shift at the factory. He took it out mainly on Todd, who was big and could be clumsy, screaming constantly at him to leave us in peace.

Bruce had a terrible temper but he'd never lost it with me. That changed in the seventh month of my pregnancy as I finished decorating our baby's bedroom. I was told by a doctor that I was expecting a girl and wanted everything to be just right for the big arrival. I called to Bruce to help me carry the paint tins back down the stairs. Out of nowhere, he started shouting at me, yelling abuse.

'I don't want a fucking child,' he screamed. 'What about me, you selfish bitch?'

He ran up the stairs, got in my face and demanded to know why he was being ignored, starved of affection. I told him to drop it and tried to get out of his way. He shoved me hard. My legs gave way and I tumbled to the bottom of the stairs, landing hard on my side. Bruce was with me in an instant, apologising.

He'd never been violent before and I didn't want to believe he was becoming abusive. I wanted to believe it was just an accident but I couldn't get over the fact that he'd hurt me, and possibly the baby we'd tried so hard to conceive. That night, I sobbed myself to sleep, praying to God my baby would be OK.

Then there was sex: Bruce wanted to make love two or three times a day. As the birth date neared I couldn't fulfil his needs. He started to disappear at odd times. I was convinced he was having an affair, although he denied it time and again.

I'd suffered menstrual bleeding throughout my pregnancy and feared I could lose my baby. I was always at the doctor's office demanding to hear the heartbeat. On 13 October my waters broke. Bruce's Aunt Edna rushed me off to St Joseph's Sisters' Hospital, an old Catholic institution on Cathedral Hill. I had mild contractions that lasted on and off for most of that day and the next.

Finally, the labour pains began in earnest. They continued for the next seventy-two hours. I didn't know it but I had toxicoma blood poisoning. I remember holding a nurse's hand and counting spots on the ceiling to take my mind off the contractions. Doctors rarely did Caesareans back then. Instead, after sixty hours in labour, I was offered some medicine in a paper cup.

I heard a nurse shouting at me, 'You're both going to die if you don't push, Debbie.' Then I recall someone saying it was a boy. But that was it: I blacked out.

I'd starting having a seizure and fell into a coma in the recovery room. This lasted for several days until the sound of a ringing bell brought me round. My eyes slowly focused on the shape of a man in black, waving a bell. He was a priest and apparently he'd given me the last rites. As I awoke a nurse grabbed my arm and started to take my blood pressure, and gradually I became aware of lots of noise and commotion all around me. It was enough to make me want to go back to sleep, until someone brought in my baby. I had a baby son!

I saw the faces of my aunts, my mother, my brothers Steven and Todd. They were all crying. Dr Claude Dumont was sitting at the end of the bed with an unlit cigar in his mouth – you could smoke in hospitals then.

'You gave everyone a bit of a scare,' the doctor said. 'We didn't think you were going to make it.'

Bruce was missing when I came to. He'd gone off to celebrate the baby's birth – I found out later – with one of my friends. They were having an affair. But at that stage all I wanted to do was see my baby.

The nurse handed me a tiny bundle and said his name was Marshall Bruce Mathers the Third. Bruce had named him when everyone thought I wasn't going to make it. We hadn't discussed it but I didn't mind. I loved my father-in-law – the original Marshall B. Mathers – and thought it was a privilege to call my child after him.

Marshall was so tiny: he weighed just 5 pounds 2 ounces (about 2.3 kilos). He had a blister bubble between his eyebrows. He had long dark eyelashes and a few tufts of blond hair. He was the most beautiful baby I'd ever seen and I was filled with overwhelming love. He was mine and no one was going to hurt him.

27

Dr Dumont charged $90 for prenatal care, the delivery and Marshall's circumcision. I was worried we'd be charged more because of my coma and blood poisoning. But Dr Dumont just kept repeating he was glad I'd survived.

Todd, who was 10, was jumping up and down. He and Steve had seen a shooting star outside in the sky just moments after Marshall was born and he wanted to drag me out of bed to see if it was still there.

Years later when Marshall was first famous he told me not to believe everything I read about him in the media. I laughed because his very first mention – in the 'Hello, World' births section of the St Joseph newspaper – was wrong. It said he was born on 16 October instead of the 17th at the Methodist Hospital.

Marshall himself added to the confusion when he hit the big time in 1999 and his record company shaved a couple of years off his age. One of his staff once called me when they were trying to update his biography. Marshall thought he'd been born in Kansas City, sixty-odd miles away.

Recently I was going through some old St Joseph newspapers and found Marshall's horoscope for the day he was born. For Tuesday, 17 October 1972, it said, 'You have a great love of color and beauty but you are practical enough to realize that, unlike many other Librans, you probably could not commercialize art to any great extent. You would do much better in the theater, where you could shine as an actor.'

It also suggested the future Eminem was 'endowed with a great sense of justice, would make an excellent jurist, arbitrator or mediator'.

All these years later it's hard to imagine my son as a keeper of the peace. His early career consisted of dissing me, his wife and his musical rivals. He also turned his love of the arts into a multimillion-dollar empire. But the astrologer got one thing right. From the moment he was born, my son Marshall was a beautiful actor. He knew exactly how to look at me from under his long dark eyelashes and put on a show.

# CHAPTER FOUR

Marshall was two months old when Bruce suggested we move to his home town of Williston, North Dakota. He was sick of my family and I had to agree. Mom was interfering as usual. She'd given birth to her sixth child, Ronnie, a couple of months before Marshall was born and constantly compared my child-rearing skills unfavourably with her own.

Bruce was offered his dad's job as assistant manager at the Plainsman Hotel in Williston, where his mom Rae also worked as a bookkeeper. My father-in-law had heart problems and was being forced to retire early.

I knew no one except my in-laws but everyone was so welcoming that I felt at home almost immediately. During my childhood we'd moved many times, so I had no qualms about starting over in a new place even though I missed my brothers terribly and worried about them all the time.

Williston's a tiny town, 30 miles from the Montana border and famous only for the crossing of the Yellowstone and Missouri Rivers. At first we lived with Bruce's parents until I found us an apartment and I got a part-time job as a cashier at the Red Owl grocery store. Everyone loved Marshall. He was so cute I entered him in bonny-baby competitions. He was seven months old when he won $100 in a Gerber Baby Food contest.

Bonnie and a friend came to visit and we went on a day trip over the border into Canada. All went well until we tried to return. We had drivers' licences but no identity papers for Marshall. Immigration officers took him away. We could hear him crying in an adjoining room. I, too, was in floods of tears. The officials said they had to check hospitals and police reports to make sure we hadn't abducted him. We finally got him back four hours later. I couldn't stop kissing his tearstained cheeks as we drove back into the United States. It was such a horrible ordeal that I vowed never to leave America again.

I sang to Marshall all the time and made up silly alternative rhymes to his nursery rhyme and Mother Goose books. 'Jack be nimble, Jack be quick, Jack jumped over the stupid candlestick' was one that made Marshall smile. He loved hearing the hymns in church on Sundays, so I sang those to him at home too. His favourite was 'The Old Rugged Cross'. He'd reach up and touch my face. If I attempted to sing something else he'd shake his head and put his hand across my mouth. I tried 'Amazing Grace' but he didn't like that at all.

The women at church asked me to join the choir but I was too shy. Anyway, Bruce always wanted me to be home. He got furious when Marshall cried, claiming I spent all my time with him. Sometimes he'd storm in, put Marshall in his playpen, then pin me down on the couch and demand I ask him how his day had gone.

He started drinking heavily and doing drugs. He didn't bother to hide it from me. He invited friends over but if I complained he just turned the music up louder. I was forever finding empty whisky and Bacardi bottles in the cupboard under the kitchen sink.

The physical violence started within weeks of our arrival in North Dakota. He came screaming into the house one evening and ordered me to put Marshall into his playpen. Then he grabbed me by the hair and slammed my face into the wall.

'Cook me a meal, bitch,' he chanted over and over as he bounced my head off the wall. Then he threw me into the kitchen. Crying, I quickly reheated the dinner I'd made for him earlier and put it on the table in front of him. He threw it on the floor.

'Now clean up the mess, bitch,' he ordered.

As I got down on my hands and knees to pick everything up he started kicking me. Then he stormed out and went drinking. This became a pattern, although he alternated between slamming my face into walls and

33

pinning me on the sofa to punch me. Every week I had to pretend I'd walked into a door or tripped over to explain the marks on my face. I must have seemed like the most accident-prone person ever.

John, who ran the grocery store, didn't buy my excuses. He urged me to leave Bruce and move in with his family. I insisted nothing was wrong but John said, 'If I see you with a black eye or busted lip again, I will hurt Bruce.'

Once, I was actually working on the cash till when Bruce stormed into the store and yanked me by my arm outside. John kept telling me to go to the police, but I was too scared. The Matherses were important people in Williston.

Bruce's mother didn't like me. She'd long ago picked her idea of a bride for Bruce and I wasn't it. But my father-in-law, Marshall Sr, was wonderful. He'd had open-heart surgery and was becoming frailer by the day, but his eyes always lit up when I arrived with baby Marshall.

One day in the summer he was sitting in the garden in a big old lounge chair when he asked me to move closer to him. I'd learned to mask my bruises with make-up and thought I hid my injuries well. But Mr Mathers knew otherwise.

'Bruce is my son,' he said, as tears welled up in his eyes. 'I love him. But I'm so ashamed of him. I can't stand the fact that I've brought up a son who beats women. I didn't raise him this way.

'I beg you, on my deathbed, that you please leave my son. Take the baby and go. Get out while you can.'

He held his arms out to me. We hugged and I told my father-in-law that I loved him. He was still tall, like Bruce, but he was skin and bones. He knew he was dying.

He was a hard worker all his life and was not the sort of man to just sit in a chair all day. Even when he'd been told not to do any manual labour as his heart couldn't take it, he still tilled the big yard at the back of his house. I truly admired him, he was a lovely man. Bruce and his mom made it very clear I was not welcome at his funeral.

Bruce's drinking, cheating and abuse got worse after his father died. When Marshall was released from hospital after treatment for pneumonia I took him to the hotel to see his daddy. I thought Bruce would be pleased but I found him with a receptionist called Heather giggling over a copy of *Playboy* magazine. They were rubbing each other. I cleared my throat and they turned round. Bruce went berserk, ordering me to leave. I drove home crying. He still didn't care even when his son was ill.

He returned a couple of hours later after walking home in the rain. He took his shoes off at the door and threw them at me. I tried to make sure Marshall was out of harm's way but Bruce grabbed him, dumped him in his playpen and screamed, 'That fucking little brat can wait!'

Then he threw another shoe at me, hit me in the face and used my stomach as a punchbag.

On my nineteenth birthday in January 1974, Bruce had

35

to work late. He gave our friend Kenny, who I worked with, $20 to take me for a meal at the Stateline Club. I didn't want to go but Bruce insisted. It was a 45-minute drive away and when we arrived the place was packed. I suggested we take our food and return home hoping Bruce would already be there. But Mary, a friend who was babysitting Marshall, said Bruce had gone out looking for me.

He returned home in the early hours of the next morning. When I asked where he'd been, he accused me of having an affair. Then he grabbed me by the hair, dragged me out of our apartment and up the stairs. He pounded my head off the neighbour's door. Then he smashed my head into the door over and over. Every time I fell forward he hit me again. This continued until he knocked me out.

The next thing I remember was Bruce slapping my face. Not nastily. He was scared.

'I thought I'd really killed you this time,' he said.

There was blood everywhere. My nose was shattered. Bruce had knocked me out cold. As always he was apologetic. He insisted he loved me, that he was under pressure at work, that he didn't know what had come over him.

I told him, 'I hate you. I'm not going through this again. I'm leaving. Just go to your mother's.'

For once he didn't argue back. I think even he realised that this time he'd gone too far. He left and a friend drove me to hospital, where I spent the next two hours trying to convince the staff that it was safe for me to go home to my baby. I had a serious concussion but I told the nurses that I had someone at home who would wake me every few hours to make sure I was OK.

Long ago I'd made a promise to God that I wouldn't allow a child of mine to be around violence, drugs or alcohol. My siblings and I had suffered enough. I didn't want my son growing up in the same environment. Marshall was fourteen months old, too young to understand what was happening. But even he had started to point at the marks on my face and say, 'Boo, boo.' It broke my heart.

I barely slept and the moment Marshall woke up I gathered up a few of his clothes and a bag of diapers. I stuffed everything into a duffle bag. If I'd been thinking straight I'd have cleared out the envelopes where we kept the rent and electricity money. But I just took a $20 note to add to the handful of dollars in my pocket. I didn't even take the car, even though it was in my name and I had almost finished paying off the loan. I went to the grocery store where I worked to pick up my check, hand in my uniform and say goodbye.

John, my boss, begged me to stay but I just wanted to get as far from Williston as possible. Kenny, one of the other workers, drove me to the railway station. There was a train leaving for Kansas City, a day and a half's journey away. From there, it was just 60 miles to St Joseph.

I was hysterical, terrified Bruce would come looking for me. He'd threatened to kill me many times if ever I tried to leave him. I'd never been on a train before and when two policemen boarded I expected them to drag me off and return me to Bruce. But they just nodded in my direction. I had a fractured nose, two black eyes and bumps on the back of my head. One woman asked me if I'd been in a car wreck. I just nodded. I didn't want to talk to anyone.

It was freezing cold and, even though we were both bundled up in winter clothes, our hands were like blocks of ice. I couldn't stop my teeth chattering. But at least we had the carriage to ourselves because everyone else had moved to warmer carriages.

A ticket conductor came through. He told me the heating had gone out, and that I had to move. Eventually, we moved into the buffet car. I gave the steward my $20 bill for gravy and mashed potato and stupidly forgot to pick up the change. The man thought it was a tip. Then Marshall got tummy ache and even though I rubbed his stomach, he cried off and on for the rest of the journey. By the time I arrived in Kansas City, sometime around two o'clock the next morning, I had just enough money to phone Mom.

Needless to say, she didn't welcome me back with open arms. She shouted something about being woken up, said there was a big snowstorm in St Joe and no one could drive out to get me. She told me to call back at a more civilised time. I sat in the station for what seemed like hours until a policeman appeared.

'Are you Debbie?' he asked.

I shook my head. Surely Bruce hadn't tracked me down already?

'It's OK,' he said. 'Your mom called us. She's going to wire some money to you for a bus ticket. Let me drive you to the terminal.'

I was so tired and hungry – if only I'd been thinking more clearly, I would have cashed my paycheck before I left. The bus station was deserted except for one clerk, who took pity on me when I told him I was waiting for money to get home.

When I asked him where the restroom was, he said: 'Come downstairs with me.'

I followed him. Hopefully there'd be a warm office and maybe some food there.

'You're very pretty,' he said, with a leer. 'We can work something out.'

I ran into the bathroom where a woman overheard me enquiring about prune juice for my son's tummy ache, and she found me some. I gave her my change – about 72 cents. Eventually I got Marshall to stop crying just before we boarded the bus. What a relief – my baby was making himself sick and I felt so helpless. I finally got home to St Joseph at 4 p.m. Mom didn't even acknowledge my bruises.

'I really liked Bruce,' she said, as though everything were my fault. 'How long are you going to stay?'

'Just a week or two, promise,' I said. I didn't even last that long. Bruce kept phoning, and there were more deeply unpleasant dramas with Mom, so I moved in with Nan, who by then was also living in St Joe.

Nan urged me to take Bruce back, too. She didn't realise he'd changed so much. She said he kept calling, crying down the phone. Eventually I agreed to talk to him.

He told me to get my ass home, adding that I could bring 'the kid' with me.

'The kid has a name,' I said.

I asked if he could send some of our clothes. He refused. I'd made Marshall several baby books, full of photos, listing things such as his favourite toy frog and his beloved cherry vanilla pudding. Bruce wouldn't even mail those back to me. The next time I saw those baby books was when Marshall was famous. They popped up in a German magazine, alongside an interview with Bruce claiming he'd searched high and low for us but we'd disappeared.

I wanted Marshall to have a relationship with his father because I remembered the pain I went through when my dad left. But Bruce didn't want to know. After just a few weeks, the phone calls stopped. I set about making a new life. I knew I had to make it alone, for Marshall's sake.

I filed for divorce but Bruce held that up by telling the clerk and my mom that I was not a resident of Missouri for the legally required six months. Eventually he was ordered to pay Marshall $60 a month in child support but he only ever paid two or three times. Finally he took off to California to avoid having to pay anything at all.

# Chapter Five

I found a tiny apartment, got a job at a restaurant and signed up to study at beauty school. Bruce's Aunt Edna helped me care for Marshall. Every night when I came home, there'd be a smiley-face drawing or cardboard model waiting for me from Marshall. He loved to draw. He was also a born showman. At kindergarten, he played an Indian in a Thanksgiving play. His Uncle Ronnie, who was just two months older, was a pilgrim.

Marshall loved hearing stories about America's history and was intrigued by the Wild West. Living in St Joseph, an old frontier staging post for cowboys, provided the perfect setting to learn about those things. It's known as the town where the Pony Express began and where the outlaw Jesse James met his end.

Until 1860, letters from New York took 30 days – via steamship – to reach California. A group of ambitious businessmen set out to prove they could provide the same service more quickly by using relays of horses and riders. It took just 10 days for post from St Joe to reach the gold-rush shantytowns near Sacramento. But, despite capturing the imagination of Americans and proving invaluable at the start of the Civil War, it went bankrupt in just 19 months, losing its owners a then spectacular $500,000. Then, in 1882, Jesse James was shot dead by his partners in crime, Bob and Charlie Ford, at his hideout on Lafayette Street. Marshall loved visiting St Joe's downtown historical district to view the bullet hole in the wall at James's house.

Marshall was a perfect baby who rarely cried. But as a child he developed a temper, just like his father. If he couldn't get his own way, he'd lie on the floor screaming. I gave in to him all the time. He was all I had. I loved him so much. I wanted to shelter him from the world and I wouldn't hear anyone say a word against him. People said I should spank him, but I don't believe in hitting children.

Tantrums aside, he was shy around strangers. I had to go outside with him to make him play with other children. For several years he preferred the company of his imaginary friend Casper. He didn't really watch *Casper the Friendly Ghost* much on TV, and he was mad about superheroes such as Spider-Man – but I guessed he got the idea for his imaginary friend from the show. He said Casper could walk through walls and would scold me for almost sitting on Casper. Marshall couldn't understand why I couldn't see Casper too.

My nickname for him was 'Mick' – lots of people called him that rather than Marshall.

I tried to make up for the fact Marshall didn't have a father by giving him everything he wanted. I never said no to him. At McDonald's I always let him have two Happy Meals – he wanted the free toys more than the food. He collected figurines – Spider-Man, the Hulk, the He Men, GI Joe, Batman and Robin. He charged around the apartment in a cape and mask, interchanging between playing Batman and Robin. He loved comic books full of cartoon heroes and copied them into his own colouring books. One Christmas he asked for an extravagant Caped Crusader costume with all sorts of accessories, including a Batmobile. I forget the exact price but it was hundreds of dollars. I tried to save up for it because I really wanted him to be happy, but it was just too much money.

I held down numerous jobs, from working in stores and waitressing to driving an ice-cream van, so Marshall could have a good life. I got jobs to fit in with Marshall; he often came with me to work.

Even when I briefly joined a group called Daddy Warbucks singing backing vocals, Marshall came with us on the road. We were a big band of hippies and there was always someone to watch over him when we were on stage. We played Ramada Hotels and Holiday Inns but I never got over my stage fright. The bigger the crowd, the worse I became. I used to stand with my back to the audience, staring at the drummer, whom I had a secret crush on.

I had lots of men friends. I went out with doctors and lawyers because I wanted to better myself. But compared with the sophisticated girls they usually dated, I felt inferior and inadequate. I lacked a four-year college degree, I didn't think I was pretty and I hated being paraded around in gowns at prim and proper functions.

I had my heart broken by always getting too close. I was looking for the perfect soul mate and dad for Marshall. I always mothered my men friends and hoped I could change them to become my idea of perfect. I was also very jealous, which caused me to lose men, especially the ones who were funny, hard-working and good to my son.

Charlie was my first serious boyfriend after Bruce. He was a great guy. He worked on the railroad in Missouri and would be back at weekends. We had lots of fun together, making wooden frames for water-beds. Marshall seemed to care a lot about him, and my brothers Steve and Todd got on with him too. All was well, except we both found it hard to trust each other totally, and eventually our mutual jealousies ruined it.

I met Don the taxi driver upon moving to Michigan. We lived together for a year, but he had a fiery Italian temperament and was insanely jealous. Our relationship unravelled when we went to the Florida Keys. Marshall got badly sunburned, his skin bubbled up so that he looked like an alligator. Don tried to stop me tending to him; he was even envious of the attention I gave my son. I left him the moment we returned home.

A few weeks later I met Curt Werner. He was three years younger than I was and five-foot-nine with coal-black hair and big brown eyes. He was totally wild and loved motorbikes. We became friends.

One night we were driving back from the movies when we noticed Don's cab had caught fire and burned out. We thought nothing of it until Don blamed me, saying I'd set it on fire. Curt jumped out of the car, ordering Don to get away from me. I couldn't believe he'd blamed me – I would never have done such a thing, not least as I knew how hard he'd worked to pay for that car.

My sister Tanya, who was 13, ran away from home. Mom put up wanted posters all over town and blamed me. She told the police I was hiding her. It's true: I knew exactly where she was, but I wasn't going to let Mom find her and beat her half to death.

Mom decided Curt was OK. We'd been dating less than three months when she encouraged us to get married. Big mistake – we barely knew each other. But he was gorgeous, he loved me and was great with Marshall. My son was my whole world, so it was important that Marshall liked him too.

The wedding ceremony was a low-key affair at a pastor's house. I wore a pretty summer dress; Curt was in jeans. Then we went back to Mom's for the reception.

That was mistake number two. Curt liked a drink and he was soon drunk.

I escaped early with Marshall, leaving Curt at the reception.

The following day Curt and I had a huge argument. Early on, I'd spelled out to him that I didn't want alcohol around my child. I'd seen the damage it had done to my family. But he ignored my wishes and kept on drinking. He said no one was going to tell him what to do in his own house.

Two weeks after our wedding, Curt took off on his motorbike and didn't come back that night. I left the next morning.

Marshall, who'd heard stories about his father from his Great-Aunt Edna, suddenly started asking about his daddy. Edna eventually gave me an address in California and Marshall spent hours writing a letter. Every day he waited for the mail to arrive, hoping his dad would write. His envelope finally came back with the words 'Return to sender, no such person' scrawled across the front in Bruce's handwriting. I didn't tell Marshall I recognised his father's hand.

Marshall loved animals so I filled our home with pets. He caught snakes and put them in my bed for a joke. One day I came home to discover his guinea pig wrapped in plastic clingfilm in the microwave.

'He's cold, I'm warming him up,' Marshall said, as I switched the oven off.

The guinea pig wasn't cold: he was dead. Marshall was

distraught as I explained his pet had gone to heaven. He insisted we bury him properly, in a shoebox with little holes cut into it so the guinea pig could breathe on his way to the afterlife.

Marshall didn't always understand just how delicate some creatures were. When he was 7, I turned my back for a second at the doctor's office and he dropped a book into an aquarium.

'That little monster has killed all the fish!' I heard an old lady shout.

Mortified, I pulled the book out of the tank, then offered to replace the fish, assuming they were just cheap goldfish. It turned out they were worth between $100 and $200 each. Trust Marshall to kill the expensive ones!

The word *monster* was bandied about many times by other people to describe Marshall. I lost my job in a store after he knocked down a display shelf, then spread-eagled himself across an aisle screaming.

'Get that damn monster out of here, now!' the manager ordered. I tried to defend Marshall, saying he was only a child. But the manager was having none of it. 'He's not a kid: he's a monster,' he said.

I had a falling-out with my best friends, Bonnie and Theresa, when Marshall pulled an old woman's hair and threw food about in a restaurant where I worked. They said he was a brat who needed spanking, but I wouldn't hear a word against my son.

School was a problem, too. Marshall hated it. He was small for his age, so he was bullied from day one. He was a great actor, constantly pretending his leg hurt or his belly ached. I spoiled him rotten, giving him everything he wanted, including days off school.

He clung to me when I dropped him off at school and panicked if he thought I was going anywhere without him. Once, he saw me putting laundry in the car, thought I was leaving and ran screaming towards the house. He was in such a state that he put his arm through the glass door as it closed. I grabbed a large towel and ran to put pressure on his arm. It was obvious to me (and later verified in hospital) that he had come very close to cutting the main artery in his wrist – it was a really close call and I was so scared. There was blood everywhere. I rushed him to hospital. He needed twelve stitches and still has the scar today.

# CHAPTER SIX

St Joseph enjoyed a mini tourist boom in the 1970s sparked by *Paper Moon*, the Depression-era black-and-white movie starring eight-year-old Tatum O'Neal and her father Ryan as Bible-selling con artists. Peter Bogdanovich used several downtown locations, as well as the Missouri River Bridge. Tatum became the youngest person ever to win an Oscar and the movie remains one of my favourites. It captures St Joseph's small-town charm, something I'd always loved. But by 1979, with a second failed marriage behind me, I needed a change of scenery.

Salvation appeared in the form of Nan. She lived in Warren, Michigan, with her partner Johnny, and needed help. Grandpa Johnny, as we called him, was seriously ill with diabetes and Nan had heart problems. Nan wrote me a letter to ask if I'd help look after them. I was working as a certified nurse's assistant at a Methodist hospital at the time. Nan had always been there for me, especially when I was young, so I quit my job straight away and that night I packed up the car and Marshall and I set off for our two-day cross-country trip. We sang all the way. A new life beckoned.

Warren is a big sprawling suburb a few miles from downtown Detroit. In the 1950s and 1960s the population had gone from just 727 people to 89,426. The population doubled again, to 179,260, in the 1970s. The reason for this expansion was what is known in history as 'white flight'. As African Americans moved into Detroit, the white families moved out. Detroit's main thoroughfares are all mile markers, hence the names 6 Mile, 7 Mile, 8 Mile and so on. For the most part, 8 Mile is a nondescript dual carriageway dotted with gas stations and small shopping malls that splits Detroit from Warren and the outer suburbs.

We moved around more than I wanted to. Every time I redecorated a house, the landlord admired it and decided to sell. This happened at least three times until I stopped letting the landlords in to inspect my handiwork. We lived in nice neighbourhoods; we were never white trailer trash. I was fastidious about my homes. They were always spotless and Marshall had everything his heart desired.

I'd always wanted a big family and felt Marshall would be less shy if he had siblings. We used to drop off his old toys at the Catholic Children's Charity. One day we were chatting to a social worker, who introduced us to three little sisters, Barbara, Wendy and Tammy. They were 14, 12 and 7 and had been pushed around foster homes for most of their lives.

I didn't know it then but the girls were distantly related to me on Nan's side. As we tried to leave, Wendy, who was considered to be slow, grabbed my leg and wouldn't let go. I offered to let them stay for a holiday. Before I knew it, they were living with us full-time along with their five-year-old brother Eric.

At last I had the big brood of children I always wanted. I had a medium-sized two-bedroom house with a half-acre of land at the back. I partitioned off the utility room to turn it into a bedroom for the girls. We had two Dobermann dogs, a ferret, several hamsters, and later on goldfish and even baby turtles, and the house was full of children's voices. The only person who wasn't happy was Marshall. He was so jealous of the attention I gave the others.

I often came home from my job as a doctor's receptionist to discover the children crying outside. Marshall had locked them out. He refused to play with them. Every evening we all sat in a circle on the floor to discuss our problems but Marshall wouldn't let me sit next to anyone but him. Sometimes he stormed off outside and wouldn't come back in until I retrieved him. Eventually, he blurted out what was really bothering him.

'You love them more than me,' he said, bursting into tears.

I took him in my arms and told him, 'I love you, you're my natural son, my whole world. If these other kids go away you'll be lonely and you will miss them. Can I be their mom, too?'

'No,' he said. 'You can be their sister or something.'

Marshall did not want to share me but, after our little chat, there was an uneasy truce. He demanded to speak about his day first when we sat in our circle. He glowered and pulled faces, snatching his toys away if they wanted to play with him.

At first Wendy was withdrawn. She rocked backwards and forwards sucking her thumb, but gradually she opened up. She copied everything Marshall did, refusing to wear a dress because she wanted jeans like Marshall. Before long she was chattering away with the others and even wearing skirts. I loved nurturing those kids. Barb, the eldest, could be rebellious, threatening to sleep in the garage with the Dobermanns or run away if she didn't get her own way, but generally we were a big happy family.

Life wasn't easy. I received no money, just food stamps and free medical care for the foster kids. But I hated using the stamps, so we played pretend Monopoly money with them before we spent them.

I shopped at Samra's Meat Market. The owner, Mr Samra, was lovely. One day he said he wanted me to meet his son Fred Jr, who'd recently got divorced.

A week or so later, I was leaving the Meat Market laden down with bags of shopping and all the kids in tow when a good-looking guy offered to help. He introduced himself as Fred.

'How many children do you have?' he asked, eyeing Marshall, Eric and the three girls.

'Five,' I said.

'Wow, that's a lot,' he said. 'I can't believe you have so many. You look so young.'

'Only one's my natural child,' I told him. 'I care for the others.'

Fred appeared impressed. His marriage had been childless but he was like a big kid himself. He was full of fun, an absolute scream to be around.

We went out to dinner just once before he got to know the children for real. He was so good with Marshall. They played football together. Fred liked a Martini or two after work and once fell out of a tree he'd drunkenly clambered up in a race with Marshall.

Fred was dark with a beautiful olive complexion. He was sturdily built but tiny in stature, not more than five-foot-three tall. I used to tease him because he wore heeled shoes to make himself look taller.

He asked me to marry him constantly but I always refused. I loved him dearly and didn't see the point of marrying again. Apart from his drinking, which he tended to do secretly, we were happy.

We went on road trips. Fred was as excited as Marshall when we saw Niagara Falls for the first time. They couldn't wait to get sprayed with water right underneath the Falls. We also drove to Tennessee and stayed in a lovely hotel in the Smoky Mountains. On other occasions we took off in the car and just stopped wherever we fancied.

The only blip was Fred's mother, who did not approve of me and constantly told Fred that he didn't need a ready-made family. But we tried to ignore her interfering.

Marshall called Fred 'Dad'. He'd never done that with any of my previous men friends. In reality, they were a pair of big kids together. For the first time I felt as if I had the large, happy family I'd always wanted.

Marshall and I often said, 'Every time something good happens to us, something bad does, too.'

Sure enough, the house caught fire.

I was on my way back home from work when I saw smoke pouring out of the windows. Marshall and the sisters were inside. I charged in, hauled them out, then grabbed the phone to dial 911. The phone literally melted in my hand. I was overcome with smoke but managed to stagger outside. I was hospitalised for several hours with carbon monoxide poisoning, and the kids also had to be checked. Thankfully they were OK.

The smoke and water destroyed everything we owned. The foster kids went back into care. We had no clothes, no furniture and nowhere to stay. Fred took off back to his parents. He was useless under pressure, and I was left to pick up the pieces. Although I managed to salvage a few of our things, the house was uninhabitable and we had to find a new place to live.

# CHAPTER SEVEN

In 1981 when Marshall was nine I enrolled him at Dort Elementary School, in Roseville, Michigan. He was tiny for his age and, as the new kid on the block, he was once again a target for bullies. His worst tormentor was DeAngelo Bailey, a big black kid from Detroit, who was two years older. I didn't know it then but Bailey used to put his head down, scuff his feet, roar and then charge like a bull at Marshall.

The first incident happened on 15 October, two days before Marshall's tenth birthday. Marshall came home in tears with a busted lip and bruised nose. He wouldn't tell me who'd attacked him. He just said it was a big, older boy. He'd been badly winded and was throwing up. I called the school principal to complain, then spent the night lying on my son's bed as he tossed and turned.

A month later Marshall again came home complaining he'd been beaten up by the same boy. Again, he wouldn't tell me the bully's name. He was terrified. Again, I called the school, begging the staff to look out for my son. Marshall started having really bad nightmares. He'd wake up screaming that the big boy was beating him. Trying to coax him to school was heartbreaking. He would just start yelling. Then he'd say he was ill, that his leg hurt or his stomach ached. I spent hours trying to talk to him about what had happened. But still Marshall would not tell me the boy's name.

Just before Christmas Marshall again came home crying. This time he'd been beaten up really badly. He had cuts and scratches all over him. It looked as if he'd been in a fight with a cat. I was at my wits' end. Again, I screamed at the school to do something.

I couldn't stand to see my son in so much pain. He'd always hated school, using bullying as an excuse for days off, but usually things improved when he stopped being the new boy. I hoped this would be the case with Dort Elementary.

I always collected Marshall from school, but on 13 January he didn't come running out to greet me as usual. He was nowhere to be found.

Eventually, two kids told me Marshall was in the toilets. I ran into the school, screaming out his name. I burst into the toilets and there I found him lying in a pool of blood, his body jerking. I scooped him into my arms, laid him on the back seat of the car, then rushed him to hospital. I was hysterical.

Marshall spent four days in hospital, slipping in and out of consciousness. I never left his side, except to go to the chapel and pray. His nose bled constantly; so did his ears. His vision came and went. He had the most terrible nightmares. He'd curl up into a ball and cry as I rocked him to sleep in my arms, then he'd wake up screaming. The doctors called this a 'burst of irregular activity in the brain'. It was horrible to see my son like that.

'Tell me who did this to you,' I urged him on countless occasions. But Marshall just shook his head. Clearly he was too terrified to give me the boy's name.

We saw 21 doctors over four days. There were ear, nose and brain specialists lining up to take a look at Marshall. He was suffering from cerebral concussion, post-concussion syndrome and acute post-traumatic stress syndrome. His vision was also damaged.

Eventually the doctors called me into a conference room at the hospital. They told me Marshall had suffered a slight cerebral haemorrhage.

'There's no hope,' one said. 'He'll never be the same. He needs to be institutionalised.'

'There has to be something you can do,' I begged. But the doctor just shook his head. His colleagues stood silently beside him.

I refused to accept the diagnosis. I'd fought hard to escape my horrible childhood and Marshall's father Bruce, and I wasn't going to give up on my baby. Instead,

I took Marshall home and vowed to nurse him back to health myself. He was all I had. I was not going to lose him.

At first he was like an infant. He could just about clamber onto my lap. He would curl into a ball to sleep, then wake up screaming. His nightmares were terrifying. He'd jolt awake, leap up and start pummelling pillows or tearing down the curtains. It was as though he were fighting the bully in his sleep.

I had to re-teach Marshall the simplest things. As a baby he was a fast learner, who walked before his first birthday and spoke in entire sentences at two. Now I had to show him how to put his left and right feet into the correct shoes, how to tie his laces and button his shirt. He couldn't even pour cereal into a bowl. He was also on medication to prevent seizures, keep his blood pressure stable and stop his nose and ears bleeding.

Fred took off. He didn't want to be around 'drama', as he called it. Anyway, I barely had time for him. My entire life was focused on getting Marshall better.

I couldn't work because Marshall was too ill. We had to go on welfare. It broke my heart. I'd never begged for anything before. I did my best to hold everything together, but there were many nights when I just sobbed myself to sleep.

I'd found out DeAngelo Bailey's name from Marshall's friends, but it took months before I could coax anything about him out of my son. Even though I was now home-schooling him, teaching him how to read and write all over again, he was still terrified Bailey would come after him again. I reassured him constantly that he was safe.

Slowly, he told me what had happened on 13 January. It was snowing and he was playing 'King of the Hill' with a group of pals in the schoolyard when Bailey appeared. He threw a chunk of ice at Marshall, striking him on the head. Marshall lost his balance and fell backwards through a snowdrift. He cracked his head as he hit the ground.

I decided to consult a lawyer to see what, if anything, could be done. I was going through living hell with my son and I didn't want anyone else to suffer like that at the hands of bullies. Marshall's medical bills were thousands of dollars and I hadn't been able to work while looking after him. I found a lawyer and filed an affidavit, explaining what had happened. A staff member laughed at me.

'You won't sue us. I'll say he bumped his head on the school door on the way out of the building,' he sneered.

Eventually the case was thrown out of court. The judge ruled that Michigan schools were immune from lawsuits. But I organised a petition, gathered other parents' names and did my best to make sure everyone knew what had happened to my son. Shortly afterwards the education authorities offered insurance to buy in case of an accident on school property. I like to think that my case against Dort Elementary went some way to making that happen.

Marshall also got his own back: in 1999 he named

Bailey as his tormentor in his song 'Brain Damage' on *The Slim Shady LP*. Bailey, then a sanitation worker, tried to sue Marshall for $1 million, claiming his privacy had been invaded by and that he'd become an object of hate. He said Marshall's slurs had harmed his potential career as a rap star. I was shocked when I heard this. How dare he?

# Chapter Eight

Marshall improved slowly. One day he could tie his shoelaces; the next he'd forgotten. It was terribly frustrating for him but every day he got a little bit better. Then, one morning, almost exactly a year after the attack, he shook me awake at 5 a.m. He was all excited. He'd dressed himself and made breakfast.

'Look,' he said, dragging me by the hand to prove he'd laid the table properly and poured cereal into his bowl. He'd even collected the newspaper from the doormat and laid it out for me. I had to make sure I wasn't dreaming – my prayers were finally being answered.

A few hours later he peered out the window, watching other children heading to school

'How come I can't go too?' he asked.

I was delighted. Marshall was on the mend. I phoned

his doctor with the news – I wanted to shout it to the world – and initially he was sceptical but agreed to run some more tests on Marshall in the morning. Excitedly I took Marshall in and he underwent some fresh electromyogram (EMG) and brainwave studies. His doctor couldn't believe the improvement. He simply couldn't explain it. I said that miracles never cease and he agreed that Marshall's recovery was indeed nothing short of a miracle. But he warned that another injury to Marshall's head could kill him. So I bought Marshall a football helmet and made him wear it when he went outside to play. He hated it but the other kids thought it was cool – for a while they all wanted one.

Marshall loved rollerblading, football and baseball. I encouraged him to play, to make new friends. But he was still terribly shy around strangers. Then he joined the Boy Scouts and became tight pals with a lad called Ronnie. They were inseparable. Ronnie, often with his two younger brothers in tow, loved spending time with us. I filled the house with children.

Parents often said to me, 'What are you doing to my child? He doesn't want to come home!' I never understood why they said that. All I did was let the children play, help them with their homework and cook them supper. We would also go bowling and roller-skating – only now I had become way too over-protective.

I'd always loved music. From the age of twelve I'd hung around recording studios with Bonnie and Theresa, getting excited over local bands. The radio was always on, and Marshall and I used to practise singing in front of the mirror using combs or hairbrushes as microphones.

The first concert I took Marshall to was the Talking Heads – their hit 'Burning the House Down' was one of our favourites. Everyone was smoking a cigarette and when someone passed a lit one to me I took a drag. I started coughing and passed it on. I nearly passed out; the ground swam in front of me, I felt sick. I tried to take a step but couldn't walk. The guy laughed when I asked what it was. He said it was pot, laced with an elephant tranquilliser. The show was almost over, and Marshall and I left. I wanted to crawl out, I felt so weird. A friend had to help me home.

That was the one and only time in my life I tried pot. It turned me off for ever. Luckily, it didn't put Marshall or me off live concerts.

Next we saw Stevie Nicks. Marshall loved every second of the show. He stood just in front of me jiving, singing along to all her hits, including old Fleetwood Mac numbers such as 'Rhiannon'. For someone who'd been unable to retain even the simplest of rhymes in his head after the attack, he'd bounced back like a champion.

My brother Todd had a guitar; a couple of my friends played keyboards. But Marshall wasn't interested in musical instruments. He was always humming and bouncing around to music, right from an early age – whether it was on the car-seat, on the sofa or in his highchair. And when he was tired he would bounce himself to sleep, humming as he bounced.

As he got older, he always had a beat in his head. He'd play tapes on his boombox over and over, writing rhymes.

Marshall and I wrote poetry to each other. I'd work several hours to get something just right, but he always managed to dash off a few lines at the speed of light.

The disc jockey Kool Herc introduced the Jamaican tradition of 'toasting' – firing off impromptu poetry over the top of reggae, funk and disco beats – to inner-city New Yorkers in the 1970s. 'Break-beat deejaying' – where the most danceable sections of funk songs are continuously repeated – followed. The craze became known as hip-hop. It took a few more years to go mainstream, but Marshall caught on early.

If I asked Marshall what he wanted to do when he grew up, he'd just shrug. I thought he'd make an excellent auctioneer – he fired off rhyming lyrics so fast that no one could understand him. I worried because he was asthmatic, yet he rarely paused to come up for air.

For a while he wanted to be a scientist. He was fascinated by dinosaurs for years, and had many books on the subject. He quizzed me constantly about where they had come from and why they had become extinct. Evolution intrigued him.

His other big love was Nintendo. He could beat all the other kids hands down.

Even my brother Todd, who adored Marshall and was always a father figure, constantly lectured me for spoiling him. He admitted he'd occasionally put Marshall in a headlock – when I wasn't looking – for behaving badly over food. He didn't hurt him, he just wanted to get his attention.

'Listen, sister,' Todd said. 'When you let that kid have a whole pizza, eat the centre, then just throw the rest away, that's too much even for me.'

Todd was right: Marshall was forever taking one bite of a pancake or waffle before demanding something new to eat. But, after what he'd been through, I just wanted him to be happy. I could never be cross with him. I wanted him to have anything – everything – his heart desired.

Marshall's recovery, after that first awful year, was rapid. But, despite his initial excitement about returning to school, it quickly became a problem again. I refused to send him back to Dort Elementary, but every time I enrolled him at a new school, within days he demanded to leave. He only had to hint that he was being bullied or that a teacher didn't like him and I kept him off school. I always believed Marshall, no questions asked. He seemed truly happy only when he was at home, drawing cartoon characters, reading comic books or writing poems. Then, as soon as school was over for the day, his stomach ache or whatever would miraculously disappear and he'd want to go outside to play football or basketball. I called it playing possum – after the mammal that pretends to be dead when fearing danger.

I watched Marshall constantly. I'd been overprotective before the attack and now I became worse. I'd nearly lost him once. He wasn't going to be beaten again. Marshall was always great at wrapping me around his little finger

– he knew exactly how to play to me. So, of course, when he was upset at school I sided with him. Every time he was bullied, I moved him. I never questioned him. I just wanted him to feel safe after what had happened to him. It's fair to say he attended at least twenty different schools. I only wanted my son to know I would do anything to protect and please him, and allay his fears.

The ghost of DeAngelo Bailey remained. It took Marshall a long time to get over his fear of kids who resembled him. The doctor said it was post-traumatic stress. Like Vietnam War veterans, he had flashbacks. Every time he saw someone who resembled Bailey he panicked.

In the car, he would slide down the seat or even try to open the door and run if he thought he saw Bailey. I'd quickly pull over, grab him and do everything I could to calm him down. Afterwards he would remember nothing of it, as though he'd had a blackout.

Once he was walking along a low wall with his arms held out wide. A bigger kid came towards him, doing the same thing. Marshall tumbled off the wall, screaming.

'Mom, Mom, he's going to get me,' he sobbed.

The other boy was upset, too. He couldn't understand what had happened – he was just being friendly. But Marshall was hysterical, hyperventilating, gasping for breath.

As I cradled my son in my arms, I told him, 'This awful thing happened to you, but God doesn't want you to be frightened of black people. It could have been a white person, or a yellow or green one, who did this to you.'

I asked him if he'd like to go back to play with the boy but he shook his head. I could see his fear. He wasn't ready to do that yet.

The panic attacks continued. Every time a bigger kid who bore a passing resemblance to DeAngelo Bailey approached, Marshall froze. Then the tears would start to fall.

I sought out children his own age and invited them to come over to make sure he had lots of different friends. I don't believe there is such a thing as a good or a bad child, only good or bad behaviour. I told Marshall all races had good people and some badly behaved people like DeAngelo Bailey. Gradually, his fears subsided.

# CHAPTER NINE

Fred and I got back together. Even though he had taken off when I needed him most, I forgave him. Nursing an injured child was hard enough for me, let alone Fred.

Fred agreed to attend Alcoholics Anonymous. I hoped he would learn why I got upset if anyone drank around Marshall. I was well aware that addiction was a disease that ran through my family.

I'd tried alcohol just once. It was Christmas Eve 1975, not long after I'd divorced Bruce. Todd was upset because our hard-drinking stepfather had refused his gift of whisky. So he and I sat on the bathroom floor drinking it. I spat the first mouthful out but over the course of the next few hours somehow we finished the bottle. Then I puked. I missed Christmas Day totally. Marshall got to spend the night with his uncle Ronnie, playing with their gifts that we'd opened the night before. I've never touched a drop of alcohol since. Unfortunately, the men I attract like to drink.

In fairness, Fred did most of his drinking apart from me. He'd stop off for a couple of Martinis at his parents' house on his way back from work. Or he'd take off to a bowling-alley bar with friends. But it still bothered me, and getting him into AA was a step in the right direction.

We also decided to move back to Missouri. Marshall was unhappy at first but soon his Uncle Ronnie was, once again, his best friend. They came home all excited once because they'd cut their arms, merged the blood and made a pact to be blood brothers. They were both crazy about hip-hop. Our home resounded to the sounds of LL Cool J and the Beastie Boys.

One evening, just as it was getting dark, I was grilling hot dogs and hamburgers for supper when my half-sister Betti, two other women and two guys stormed into my house. I was looking after my neighbour's baby. They snatched her from my arms, tossed her onto some carpeting, then threw my food everywhere.

Betti went for me. I was on my way inside when someone grabbed me and cracked me over the head with a beer bottle. They dragged me across the kitchen by my hair and yanked me back outside. I yelled, but Marshall, in his room with a couple of friends, had his Nintendo turned up loud.

Betti screamed, 'Bitch, you're dead!' and I was dragged across the yard and onto the pavement beside the house.

She jumped on my chest and pummelled me, while the girls held me down. Even the guys joined in, kicking me with their cowboy boots. Then they tried to drag me into their car. I remember kicking out, screaming as loud as I could.

An old man, turning into our road in his car, saw in the light from his headlights what was going on. He fired a shotgun in the air to frighten them off. They ran and jumped in their car and backed up the hill. I thought they were going to try to run me over, but instead they sped off.

Marshall appeared as the car roared off. He picked up a handful of rocks and yelled, 'Leave my mom alone!'

The man helped me into the house. I'd lost one of my sandals. My hair was in knots from the blood streaming down the back of my head. My white blouse had turned brown-red.

As I went to dial 911 for the police, the phone rang. It was my mother.

'Your daughter just beat me up,' I mumbled.

'You mean she didn't kill you,' she said. Mom was always making crazy accusations about me. Her previous partner was a city bus driver. I'd not long moved back to St Joe when he would sometimes pop in to see me. Out of courtesy I would offer him coffee. He still loved Mom, even though they'd split up. I think he hoped I could persuade her to get back with him. I told him to stay

71

away from her. I said he was like a stuck record: it was the same old drama over and over again.

The police arrived and told me to go to hospital. I had concussion, my nose was broken, I had a dislocated shoulder, three or four broken ribs and gravel embedded in the gashes on my face, arms and legs. I had also suffered a bad injury to my back, though I didn't know it at the time.

'You look like you've been run over by a train,' the doctor said.

I was an absolute bloody mess. My hair had to be cut shorter because I couldn't get a comb through the knots. Worse, I needed to wear a thick plastic brace around my torso and I couldn't even take a step forward without the aid of a walking frame. I had to learn how to walk again. One week I managed three steps, the next six. I was spending several days a week going to physiotherapy; my lovely therapist Chris Marsh kept me feeling positive during what was a really hard time. Without his and my doctor's support and encouragement I don't think I could have done it.

The court prosecutors refused to take any action against my attackers. My sister claimed I'd invited them all over for a barbecue, then I'd suddenly lunged at them with a big grilling fork. They had apparently fought me off.

Since childhood I'd been accused of all sorts of things by Mom. On an earlier occasion she took off her earrings, rolled up her sleeves and went for me.

'You're not too old for me to beat your ass,' she snarled – all because I was standing up for my brother Todd. Marshall and I had stopped by one evening after my beauty school. My Mom, stepdad and siblings were eating supper and Marshall, too young to understand, jumped up to the table. Mom immediately got up, saying that it figured I'd stop by while they were eating. Todd had offered his sandwich to Marshall but Mom yelled at him not to – so Todd headed up to his room, swiftly followed by my stepdad who demanded he come back down. I ran over to the stairs and told him not to dare touch Todd – but by this time he was trying to pull my brother down the stairs.

People who know my family are amazed at the way I turned out. By rights I should have been an alcoholic sitting on a bar stool with my kids running wild outside on the streets. Instead, I fought to be the complete opposite of that.

The last person I wanted to be like was my mom. The mother in a family is supposed to be the rock – mine was more like a piece of gravel. I don't hate my mother, because I believe it is a sin to hate. Despite everything, I still love her. But back then whatever I did was never good enough for her. I called her merely my birth mother because that was the only bit of mothering I recall she ever did for me.

When I was growing up, Mom twice attempted suicide in front of me by swallowing handfuls of pills. Once, when I went to visit her in hospital after yet another apparent failed overdose, she punched me on the nose. There was no reason for all the craziness. But Mom thrived on it. Music was my escape. And then, to make up for Mom, I gave Marshall too much love.

In the summer of 1985 I discovered I was pregnant. No one was more surprised than I was. A few years earlier I'd suffered an ectopic pregnancy – the baby had started to develop outside the womb in my left Fallopian tube, which I then lost. The doctor warned me it was highly unlikely I'd ever conceive again. Now I was expecting – and ecstatic. Unfortunately, Fred and Marshall didn't share my excitement.

Marshall was twelve and still crazy about all things prehistoric. When I asked him if he preferred a little brother or a little sister he joked, 'Why can't we have a baby dinosaur?'

Fred's reaction was even stranger. He was almost forty, he loved kids, Marshall called him Dad and this was going to be his first natural child. I was two months pregnant when his mother phoned to say she needed him back in Michigan because she was having eye surgery.

I asked Fred not to leave. But he packed his bags regardless.

'If you walk out the door, that's it. Don't come back,' I said.

But he just smiled sweetly, kissed me on the head and promised to return.

Weeks went by and he didn't come back. I phoned

Samra's Meat Market – his dad was always so lovely. He promised he'd get Fred to call. Then his mother would snatch up the phone and order me to stop calling. I heard through the grapevine that Fred was having an affair with a young girl called Tina. I phoned and phoned but he would not return my calls. I was a total wreck. I couldn't believe he had left me after almost seven years together.

I was selling Avon cosmetics door to door but, as my pregnancy progressed, it became harder to walk up and down the hills around St Joseph. I was high-risk and was not allowed to do any lifting or many household chores. I hired a friend of Theresa's family to do the chores in exchange for room and board. It worked out well for a time as I could not have afforded to pay for hired help.

Aside from his allowance, Marshall was determined to earn money too. He was mad about breakdancing, so he made a big cardboard sign, announcing it cost 25 cents to watch. Then he got me to stand in the parking lot, with the sign around my neck, holding a cup to collect the money. For some reason he would wear only white to breakdance. By the time he'd finished spinning on the ground he was filthy.

For the second time in my life I was forced to go on welfare. I hated it but had no choice. Fred wouldn't even talk to me, let alone send any money. Then, just when things couldn't get any worse, they did.

In the seventh month of my pregnancy I was talking to my brother Todd when a crazy man called Mike Harris

appeared from nowhere. He grabbed me, pulled up my
top, held a knife to my belly and growled, 'I'll cut the
baby out and hand it to you.'

I saw his eyes – they were fiery. He was clearly high on
drugs. My legs buckled underneath me. Todd beat him
off and chased him down the street. Then he helped me,
gasping for air, back into my car.

The doctor sent me to hospital, ordering me to stay
there for the remainder of my pregnancy. The baby's
food supply had somehow got cut off and he wasn't
growing properly. It was the shock of the knife attack.

A friend cared for Marshall, while I lay on my side in a
nondescript hospital room for two long months hoping
that and praying that my baby would grow and be healthy.

The six high-risk specialists gathered round my
hospital bed preparing me for the worst – there was a
chance my baby would need to be rushed off to another
hospital for heart surgery. Thank God he was OK.

Nathan Kane came screaming into the world on 3
February 1986. He had jaundice and colic, and he would
not stop crying. He was considered premature.

Marshall was not impressed.

'Send him back,' he ordered. Then as a joke he added,
'I want a baby dinosaur, not him.'

A couple of the neighbours said that at thirteen
Marshall was too old to be obsessed with dinosaurs. I
ignored them. The women said the same thing when
Marshall did his drumbeats or would breakdance over
and over. They'd try to say he was retarded. That was

76

ridiculous: he wasn't retarded, he was making music. And he'd won a poetry competition at school. His verse was displayed in the local shopping mall. I dismissed the other mothers' words as jealousy.

# CHAPTER TEN

Flushed by his poetry success, Marshall now knew exactly what he wanted to do for a living. He idolised LL Cool J and wanted to be a hip-hop artist. His peers laughed at him, but I told him he could achieve anything he wanted in life.

He scribbled lyrics over napkins, scraps of paper, even grocery-store receipts, and he woke me up constantly in the middle of the night to ask what words meant. I bought him a dictionary. He pored over it, memorising unusual words and meanings.

Marshall worried constantly about the state of the world – he hated wars, famines and poverty. He was all for peace and prosperity; his lyrics reflected those things.

He also had drawing books full of cartoon characters he'd created. He never mentioned his father, but once, when I couldn't get to his school parents' evening, he left me a drawing of himself sitting alone on the porch. It was his way of saying he was upset. When he was happy, he made me pictures of butterflies, knowing I loved them.

I got annoyed when his teachers gave him C grades for art. His drawings were so good, they accused him of copying. But he did well in music, often getting a B grade. I had Marshall prove to one of his teachers that he really could draw. They still had a hard time believing it.

He and Ronnie had silly quarrels over pop. Ronnie moved away from hip-hop and was into Bon Jovi, rock and heavy metal. So Marshall honed his rapping skills on Todd and Nan. And, despite his initial reservations, he soon fell in love with his baby brother. He cradled Nathan to sleep, gave him his bottle and mothered him to pieces.

Nathan's front four baby teeth had to be pulled after he contracted a rare bacterial infection. It was heartbreaking – he was only two and a half years old and had beautiful white teeth. His adult teeth didn't grow until he was nearly eight. Until the age of three he refused to be parted from his bottle, sucking on it even when it was empty. I tried throwing it away but somehow he always managed to retrieve it.

Fred called once: he wanted to come back. But I couldn't forgive him again. He'd left me pregnant and barefoot in the kitchen. Then his mother begged me to take him back – she didn't like his girlfriend Tina. I told her he'd made his bed and he could lie in it. There was also the issue of child support. He'd declared bankruptcy to avoid paying my hospital bills when I was pregnant. He didn't pay a penny until 1995. Even then he claimed hardships to court and I couldn't count on the money as it was $35 every two weeks and only ever came off and on. Fred continually asked for his rights to his son to be severed, which I refused as he got off lightly as it was. But he did start paying maintenance right before Nathan's sixteenth birthday.

Thank God my doctor had given me something to calm my nerves – I don't think I could have got through the many trials and tribulations without some help. I'll never forget Dr B telling baby Nathan, 'Listen, little man, when you're grown up, if you see your dad, give him a good punch on the nose for me.'

Marshall loved our duplex apartment in Savannah. It was brand new and he had the entire top floor to himself. But I remained scared that the mad man who'd attacked me when I was pregnant would return, just like Marshall after he was beaten by DeAngelo Bailey.

It was time to return to Michigan but Marshall did not want to go. He threatened to run away, begged me to let him stay behind and get a job – anything to stay in Missouri. Even though he loved Nathan he still had flashes of jealousy. He accused me of ignoring him, giving Nate too much attention. Threatening to run away was his way of fighting back. I insisted he was too young to live on his own, and asked how he was going to earn a living.

'I'll get a job in a factory or on a farm,' he said. I knew he wasn't serious – he was just rebelling.

It was a tough few weeks but eventually Marshall came round. Once we were back in Michigan he soon reconnected with his old friends and started to make new ones.

Our house was always full of kids. I joined Parents Without Partners, a group for the divorced and separated that encouraged families to get to know each other. There were picnics, lake beach parties and barbecues.

I soon fell for a landscape gardener called BJ. He had several kids but saw them only rarely. I noticed how good BJ was around my boys. They were both frightened of water and neither really wanted to learn how to swim. But BJ encouraged Nathan to splash about in the lake, wading out with him hand in hand. I was very strict about the men in my life – my kids were everything – I gauged how they treated my boys and their pets. And, of course, they had to be teetotal. BJ passed every test at the time.

BJ had been badly hurt by his last wife but that didn't stop him proposing to me after just three months. Marshall was 15 and I valued his opinion when it came to the men in my life. He told me to go for it.

We were married by BJ's minister. He was a big, surly man who asked if I was sure I wanted to go through with it. I thought that was a bit odd. He did the ceremony in a small office. I wore a long, pink, satin dress. BJ had on a suit and tie.

But there was something preying on Marshall's mind when we got home that night.

'Where's he sleeping?' he asked, glaring at BJ.

'My room,' I said.

'Oh, no, he's not!' Marshall screamed. 'He can sleep outside in his truck.'

With that, Marshall ordered BJ outside. He stood glowering in front of the door. I pleaded with Marshall not to be silly.

'We're married,' I said.

Marshall stormed off to his bedroom.

BJ spent our wedding night in his truck. I remained inside. The overprotective mother now had an overprotective son.

Marshall had a violent temper. He'd pushed me a few times. He also threatened men he thought were admiring me. Sometimes at traffic lights, he'd roll down the car window and shout at unsuspecting male drivers, 'What are you looking at? She's my mom.'

His father had been insanely jealous, too, constantly accusing me of having affairs. At the time I thought it was ironic that the cheating Bruce lashed out at me for perceived adultery. But now Marshall was exhibiting the same jealous streak. We talked throughout my wedding night. He finally let BJ back into the house the following day.

BJ was strict but I told him there was no way he was going to discipline my kids. I refused to let him raise his voice to Marshall or Nathan. Meanwhile, I smothered him in love. He'd had such an awful first marriage that I wanted him to know I truly cared about him.

We'd been married only three months when BJ started to act oddly. I invited his children over for Christmas but as we drove them home he began driving erratically. I wasn't sure what was happening but it took more than an hour to calm him down. Even his kids pleaded with him to slow down but that just made him drive faster. They were as frightened as I was.

A few days later he insisted on checking my car. He was outside with his tools for ages before he'd let me drive off. I got halfway down the road and a wheel fell off. He'd loosened all my wheels. It was winter, there was snow on the ground, and I thank God I was in a turning lane on a quiet road, and almost at a stop. On another occasion I woke up with a shadow looming over me – BJ was wielding a tree saw over me. I screamed and Marshall came flying into the room.

'What the fuck is going on here?' he shouted, as BJ backed off. He'd hidden the saw beside the couch.

I had no idea what was going on but I was starting to get very worried about the man I'd just married.

Then one afternoon he came charging into the house like a crazed maniac. He screamed that he wanted to talk but his eyes were big and glassy. He looked like a wild animal. I tried to run into the kitchen but he dragged me by the hair and started hitting my head against the fridge, followed by a couple of slaps to my face. Nathan was hollering BJ's name outside in the sandbox. I begged BJ to stop. He heard Nathan and paused for a second, before going outside. I grabbed the phone and called 911.

The police found BJ in the sandbox with a shovel, playing with Nathan and our chow dog Teddy Bear. He was acting like a little kid. Then he spat in my face as the police led him back through the house and out the front door.

Nathan was too young to understand but Marshall was furious. I wanted to die when he asked how I had got the marks on my face.

BJ was locked up by order of court in a psychiatric hospital. He'd apparently suffered a massive nervous breakdown. The doctors thought that he'd had such an awful time during his first marriage that he'd finally cracked when he met someone who truly cared for him. He couldn't believe that someone so nice, with a lovely home and children, could love him. It didn't make a lot of sense to me. I was now terrified of him. I got a restraining order to stop him coming near me, then I started divorce proceedings.

The marriage had lasted exactly three months. But BJ didn't go away easily. He was on the phone so often that no one else could ever get through. Once, Marshall snatched up the phone and told him, 'Punk, get over here so I can beat your ass. I'll fight you.'

I was working as a home healthcare assistant but I found it hard not to get over-attached to my patients. Many were handicapped or crippled; they struggled to get in and out of regular vans. I decided to become a limo

85

driver. I knew the senior citizens would prefer to have me driving them than the men who usually took them around. It was the perfect job. Nathan rode up front with me and soon I had customers requesting only me. I chatted to businessmen on the way to the airport and realised I could undercut my competition.

It was time to go it alone. I bought a 1977 white Cadillac with a plush, burgundy interior for $1,600, called the company Classic Rides Ltd Transportation Service and got myself several smart suits. The business took off. Within the year I had two more vehicles, one I'd bought from the county treasurer of Warren, whom I'd met when I worked for the Comprehensive Employment and Training Act (CETA) programme. I bought a 1979 Lincoln TC and then a 1985 Cadillac Fleetwood Brougham. I did most of the driving myself. Eventually I hired Don, a lovely senior man, and another driver who didn't work out. I had a lot of work – doing the driving, as well as all the paperwork, billing, answering the phones and so on. I joined the National Association for Female Executives and many other organisations. I was so proud; I'd finally found the perfect career. Although exhausting, I loved my new career.

I'd already decided it was about time we owned a home. Until then, I'd always rented. The house was at 19946 Dresden Street on the Detroit side of 8 Mile. The down payment was $3,000. I saved as much as I could to buy the house on a land contract from a lovely senior

*Above left*: Me aged four months.

*Above right*: My mom Betty smiling as I blow out the candles on my birthday cake, aged two.

*Below left*: My parents Bob and Betty Nelson not long after their marriage, in the mid- to late-1950s.

*Below right*: I'm looking very skinny, aged 10, after my parents had split.

*Above left*: Opening presents on my wedding day, September 1970, with my husband Marshall 'Bruce' Mathers Junior reading a message.

*Above right*: Bruce and I on our wedding day, with my maternal great grandmother and great granddad Mount.

*Below*: Bruce's father Marshall Senior is on the left and my parents Betty and Bob are on the right.

## MISSOURI

# BIRTH CERTIFICATION

DATE FILED **NOVEMBER 8, 1972**  STATE FILE NUMBER **124-72-027132**

CHILD NAME  SEX  DATE OF BIRTH  COUNTY OF BIRTH
**MARSHALL BRUCE MATHERS III**  **MALE**  **OCTOBER 17, 1972**  **BUCHAN**

MOTHER MAIDEN NAME  MOTHER AGE  MOTHER STATE OF BIRTH
**DEBORAH R NELSON**  **17**  **KANSAS**

FATHER NAME  FATHER AGE  FATHER STATE OF BIRTH
**MARSHALL B MATHERS JR**  **21**  **MAINE**

THIS IS A TRUE CERTIFICATION OF NAME AND BIRTH FACTS RECORDED IN THIS OFFICE.

*Garland H. Land*
Garland H. Land
State Registrar of Vital Statistics

ISSUED ON BEHALF OF THE MISSOURI
DEPARTMENT OF HEALTH BY KC HEALTH DEPT  **MARCH 4, 1999**

DATE ISSUED

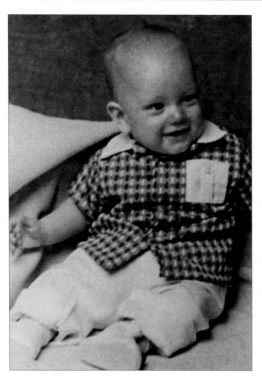

*Above*: This is a copy of Marshall's birth certificate – giving his correct date and place of birth.

*Below left*: My baby son aged three months.

*Below right*: Marshall as a toddler, aged two and a half.

*Above left*: Me, aged 22, with my 16-year-old brother Todd.

*Above right*: I made both our outfits here! Marshall is aged four.

*Below left*: Marshall at kindergarten.

*Below right*: His first school photo, aged six.

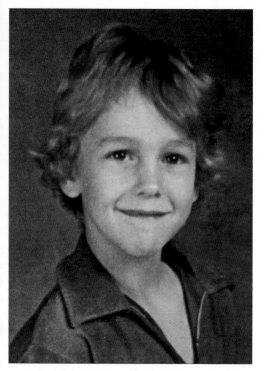

*Above left*: Marshall's best friend, his uncle Ronnie Polkingharn.

*Above right*: Marshall, school photo aged 10 or 11, not long after his recovery from the DeAngelo Bailey beating.

*Bottom left*: Easter 1983, and Marshall's holding his pet guinea pigs, shortly before he microwaved one to warm it up!

*Bottom right*: Marshall in the sea at Key West, Florida.

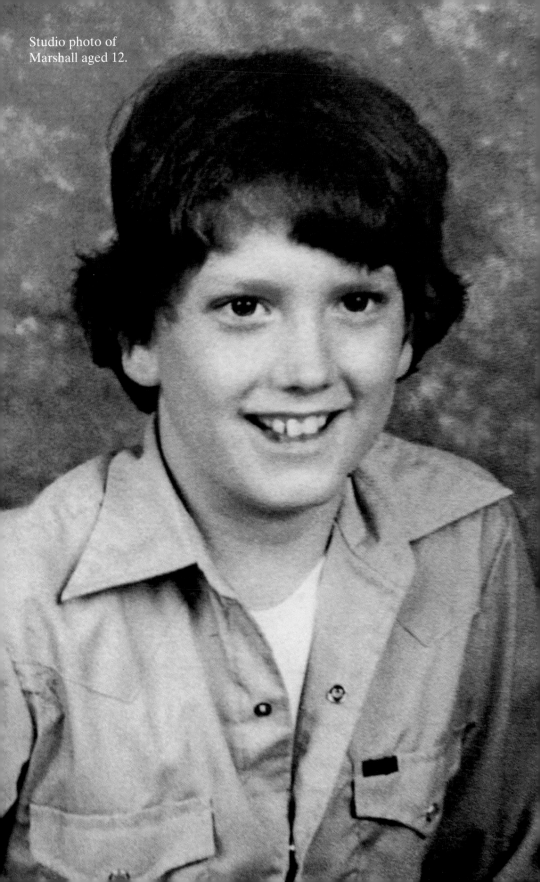

Studio photo of
Marshall aged 12.

*Above left*: Marshall with my cousin Gary Nappier.

*Above right*: Me with my two-month-old son Nathan.

*Below left*: Marshall, aged 14, holding a birthday cake.

*Below right*: Marshall holding Nathan, Warren, Michigan, October 1988.

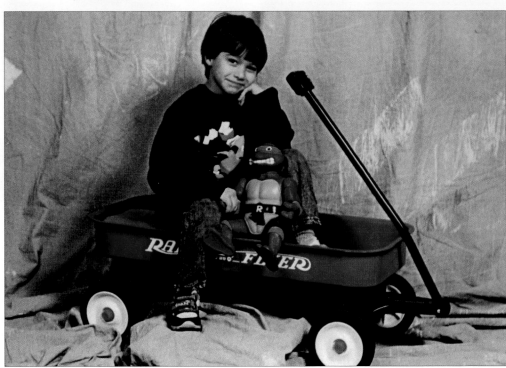

*Above left*: Marshall, aged 15, dressed in his favourite all-white breakdancing gear.

*Above right*: Bruce sent this old surfer dude picture of himself to Marshall.

*Below*: Nathan sitting on a truck at kindergarten, aged five.

couple, the Kovaleskis. When we eventually moved after five years we stayed in touch.

Years later Marshall claimed 'some dude' had bought me that house. That's simply not true. I paid for it all myself and Marshall loved it so much that he had a model of it made to take on tour with him. Even though we'd moved a lot, he always said the house on Dresden was his childhood home.

# CHAPTER ELEVEN

Marshall arrived home from school with a tall, sulky blonde girl. He introduced her as Kim Scott and said she needed a place to stay. I was happy to help out.

Kim said she was 15 and I had no reason to doubt that. In truth, she was so cute and busty that she could have passed for 17.

At first she barely spoke. Questions were answered with a shake of the head. I pampered her, lending her my clothes, showing her how to put on make-up. I treated her like the daughter I'd always wanted.

Gradually, she started to open up. She had a twin sister called Dawn, had no idea who their real father was and claimed to have been sexually abused by her stepfather. Now, as often happens with troubled children, Kim told some pretty tall tales. She'd been raped, forced to sleep with relatives on a regular basis, beaten by her mother. You name it, it had happened to Kim. My job wasn't to sort out fact from fiction: I simply listened and offered advice. I told her about my own similar experiences.

If I asked her to empty the dishwasher or do the vacuuming she'd just say no and walk off. Communication wasn't her strong point. I always picked up after Marshall. Now *she* was throwing her stuff on the floor and expecting me to clean up after *her*. I didn't mind lending her my clothes if she asked first. But she just took them. She especially liked a lacy cream top and silk skirt I owned. I'm tiny so the outfit was knee-length on me, but on Kim, who even then was almost six foot with large breasts, it looked positively obscene. She refused to give it back, claiming she had bought an identical one herself.

Why did I put up with her? I'd been fostering kids for years. Our house was full of waifs and strays. I looked on Kim as a challenge, someone I hoped I could give a better life to. After all, I'd been through the mill with my own family. Even so, I didn't trust her. Once she started to feel comfortable around me, she began to cause trouble.

Marshall had the biggest bedroom. It ran the entire length of the upper floor, but he spent most of his time in the basement – which he'd converted into a makeshift recording studio – scratching records with his pals. After a couple of months, I noticed Kim was getting grouchy around his friends. She accused one of them of coming on to her.

Marshall and I had always talked about everything. Nothing was taboo. Every evening we sat down together on the couch for a chat. Suddenly Kim started shoving herself in the middle of us. She was jealous of everyone, even Nathan.

I guessed Marshall and Kim were now boyfriend and girlfriend but assumed the relationship would burn itself out. As a precaution, I made sure she was always tucked up on the couch outside my bedroom door every night. I did not want her sneaking upstairs to Marshall.

On her sixteenth birthday, I made her a cake and we had a party. All hell broke out a few weeks later when the school phoned me to say Kim hadn't been seen in months. I explained she was sixteen; I couldn't make her attend classes.

'She's not 16: she's just turned *13*,' replied the cold voice on the other end of the phone. I felt sick. The moment Marshall walked in the door, I said, 'We need to talk.'

But he didn't want to know. He insisted she was 16, claiming she was in the same year as he was at school.

'Son, you're fifteen. She's much too young for you,' I said.

Marshall hurled a stream of obscenities at me, then retreated into the basement. Kim returned a few hours later. When she saw my face, she ran to Marshall and then he followed her out of the front door.

From that day on chaos reigned.

I did try to get on with Kim but she hated me. Her parents hated Marshall. When I had the displeasure of bumping into Kim's mom at bingo, I would sometimes hear her yelling obscenities at the winners. Kim told me all sorts of sordid stories about her stepfather Casey. I'm not sure I believe her, but I do know he frightened the life out of Marshall. When Casey found out my son didn't like water he persuaded him to go out on the lake with him in a tiny boat. Once they got away from the shore, Casey rocked it up and down, threatening to hurt him. Marshall said he'd also waved a gun at him. He was banned from even going onto their driveway.

Kim flitted back and forth between our house on Dresden and her parents' place, just off 8 Mile. There was always a drama: she claimed she'd been attacked by a crazed alcoholic paedophile; a gang of lads had jumped her in a store. She goaded Marshall into fights, ordering him to find the people who'd beaten her up. Once, Kim pointed to three burly guys in the street. Marshall confronted them, then she backtracked, saying maybe it wasn't them. I was terrified someone would pull a gun on him.

She goaded me, too. When she wasn't stealing my clothes or breaking my stuff, she bragged about her sex life with Marshall. It was horrible. In later years she boasted how she'd sneaked upstairs in those first few months to sleep with my son.

I really tried to talk to Kim. But she took absolutely no notice of me. Marshall, meanwhile, was devoted to her. She was his first girlfriend and he was like a puppy dog around her. When she had surgery on her foot, he carried her around in his arms.

When he got attacked by four guys, Kim told him, 'Take it like a man.'

I begged him to dump her. Marshall refused. It got to the point where I couldn't even talk to him if she was in the house. We had to wait until she went out. Marshall's friends, the other kids I fostered and even little Nathan understood. They would discreetly disappear to the basement the moment Kim slammed out of the door, so that Marshall and I could have time together.

'She's my girl, you're my mom. Please don't make me choose,' he said many times.

We'd always written each other poetry to explain our feelings. I still spent nights scribbling down my thoughts. Like the narrator in the Moody Blues' song 'Nights in White Satin', I wrote many letters to Marshall that I never meant to send. Writing was therapeutic. Sometimes I took an inspirational line from one of my poems and stuck it on the fridge door. 'We are born crying, we must to learn to laugh' was one. Another said, 'Children are on loan to us from God.'

Marshall stopped showing me his rhymes. Kim didn't approve. But he was messing around with stage names. His first professional name was M&M – a play on his initials. But his friends called him PW – it stood for pussy-whipped.

I know teenagers rebel and I suppose I was lucky: Marshall was a late starter. But by his sixteenth birthday he was out of control. He was angry all the time.

Kim wanted to know how she could track down her

real dad. Then Marshall started asking about *his* dad. For the first time I decided to contact Bruce. I tracked down his telephone number in California and, with shaking hands, dialled. Bruce wasn't in but his wife Lesley sounded lovely. She promised to see what she could do.

A few weeks later a letter arrived. I recognised the handwriting immediately. Marshall tore the envelope open. A short note and two photographs fell out.

> Just wanted to drop you a quick note to let you know we're really looking forward to seeing you soon. Enclosed is a recent picture of me so you'll know who to look for at the airport. I'm sure you're going to enjoy yourself out here, the weather is just great and we live right across the street from the beach so bring your trunks. Hope to see you soon.
> Dad

We studied the picture of a middle-aged, long-haired Bruce holding a birthday cake. He'd grown ugly but I could see Marshall had his chin. The other snap was of a much younger Bruce, holding a surfboard.

'Is that it?' Marshall said, throwing the letter down. He said he didn't want to go to California and I certainly didn't want to see Bruce again. Just looking at the pictures brought back memories of violence.

Marshall never mentioned his father again. But his rebellion continued. He took it out on any man who

94

dared to cross our threshold. He'd always been jealous of my male friends; now he forbade them to come through the door.

'You're my mom. I'm in charge. This is my house,' he'd say.

He was full of teenage insecurities and totally jealous. He accused me of loving Nathan more than him. Time and again, I reassured him. I love both my sons equally.

There were still flashes of the old Marshall. He continued to sign Christmas, birthday and Mother's Day cards, 'Love, your number one son, Marsh'. But the close relationship we'd always had was fractured. I couldn't help but blame Kim.

Marshall quit Warren's Lincoln High School. I only found out when he refused to get up one morning. It transpired he hadn't been in weeks.

I gave him my lovely Lincoln town car on his seventeenth birthday because he needed to get around. When Kim wound him up, Marshall pounded his fists on the car and kicked the tyres. I'd never seen a vehicle with so many dents in it.

I was terrified whenever my son left in the car. I worried about him all the time. He was forever getting pulled over by the police on Dresden. In my opinion he was being harassed, and when I made enquiries I was told they could pull him over if they wanted to. Sometimes he would be frisked and his tapes and stuff would be thrown out of the car. My dear friends across the street would call or run over to tell me they'd seen the police pull my son over again. Thank God it eventually stopped. I even tried following him a few times, just to make sure he would get wherever he was going, until he found out.

Marshall had long got over his fear of anyone resembling DeAngelo Bailey. Now most of his friends were African-Americans from the Detroit rap scene. DeShaun Holton – known to everyone as Proof – was his best friend. Brian 'Champtown' Harmon was another close friend. Marshall embraced everything about black culture. Unfortunately, not everyone understood why. He was forever getting into fights.

The call I had always dreaded came in the early hours of the morning. Marshall was in a police holding cell. He'd been driving Proof and two other pals from a recording studio when one of them leaned out of the rear window and sprayed a paint gun at some vagrants at a gas station, as they were hanging onto the car and asking for change. The police pulled them over. According to Marshall, he was hauled off in handcuffs, shoved into a cell and beaten by a black officer.

Apparently, the officer had called him a poof for wearing earrings. Then he'd put one foot on Marshall's back and said, 'I'm talking to you, boy. What colour are all your friends? What colour are you?' Marshall said the cop had shoved a handful of dirt into his mouth, then kicked him in the face.

I was furious when I discovered Marshall was the only

white kid in a police line-up. Marshall and his friends were taken to another precinct for a line-up for carjacking. The police had also impounded his car. I hired a lawyer, proved the gun was only a plastic paint-gun – and not, as charged, an assault with a deadly weapon – showed also that the Lincoln belonged to Marshall, and got the charges dropped. The case was thrown out of court. There was no mugshot to prove his bruises and because the charges against him were dismissed he did not have a criminal record. All records were destroyed as per the judge's orders.

The arrest scared Marshall. He'd never been in trouble with the police before. Now he told me he never wanted to see the inside of a police cell or jail again. I felt nothing but relief that this was over, though I was still angry about the officer's treatment of Marshall and his friends.

# CHAPTER TWELVE

In March 1990 I was driving with Nathan and a friend
called Gary through Kalamazoo, Michigan, when we
were rear-ended by a drunk driver. My throat struck the
steering wheel and took the brunt of the impact.

After a brief visit to hospital I returned home thinking
the strange lump in the back of my throat would go
away. But it got worse. Eating was impossible. My voice
went. I thought the shock of the crash had caused
laryngitis. The best I could manage was a low growl.
Somehow I'd damaged nerve endings in my vocal cords.
At the time, doctors thought they were only swollen.

I couldn't even take a sip of water without choking.

My weight plummeted to just 79 pounds (that's
around 5.5 stone, or 36 kilos). I didn't want to worry my
kids, so when we ate dinner I chewed tiny pieces of

meat, then spat them out into a napkin when no one was looking. I just couldn't swallow. Even baby food refused to slide down my throat.

Nathan, who was four, cried constantly, 'I don't want a mommy that doesn't talk.'

I communicated using a notebook and pen until gradually my voice came back. I spent countless hours with a speech therapist relearning the simplest of things, such as how to pronounce Ks and Ss. I also had to practice forming a bolus when I ate, and relearn how to swallow. The doctors called it dysphagia, and I'm told it's comparable to being a patient after a stroke, having to learn how to put food on the end of your tongue and then curl it back before swallowing twice. With no feeling at the back of my mouth, it was impossible to tell if food had gone down. I had to rely on soft and pureed foods until my dysphagia passed from acute to mild through lots of hard work. I had to use a long thin dental instrument, cooled down by being put on ice, and rub the back of my throat with it three times a day. To this day, however, I still have permanent nerve damage to my throat.

Years later, Marshall claimed I had made him quit school to care for me. That isn't true. He'd already left and was working odd jobs on building sites. But while my physical injuries slowly healed, the psychological ones did not. I started to have panic attacks. Something as easy as walking into a restaurant became impossible. I'd see people's faces – big, oversized faces – and their voices were amplified. I felt everyone was staring at me.

My chest tightened, I couldn't breathe – I had to run away. I was finally prescribed medication to help relieve my panic attacks.

To me drugs are illegal substances, like cocaine and heroin, not something the doctor prescribes. Even so, Marshall's comments and lyrics really hurt. On the song 'Marshall Mathers' he wrote that I hid pills under my mattress and in 'Cleanin' Out My Closet (I'm Sorry Mama)' he totally let rip. He blames my mood swings for our woes, claiming I was forever bitching about things going missing. Well, I blame Kim for that. She was always winding me up. A saint would have snapped trying to deal with her.

She called the police once to complain that she had found a curio cabinet that she thought wasn't mine. I had no idea what she was talking about. Nathan and I had been away on vacation and early in the morning of our first day back I was awoken by the police department asking if they could come in and look. Of course, I had nothing to hide so I welcomed that. Previously there had been a mistaken delivery to my home which, so I thought, had been resolved.

The police searched my bedroom. They looked in Nathan's closet and, sure enough, there was that damn curio cabinet. Kim laughed and said, 'Ha, ha. Busted.'

I was taken to the police station and fingerprinted. I told the officers to dust the curio cabinet for fingerprints. I knew they wouldn't find mine there. Always drama with Kim.

Not long after I started driving again, Marshall called me from Ohio, where they'd gone for a weekend to an amusement park. His friend's car had blown up. I took one of my company limos, drove with Nathan through the night and arrived at 4 a.m. Kim refused to leave. We all ended up at the amusement park for the day, agreeing to meet up at 10 p.m., so we could drive back to Michigan. I knew Kim would defy me. Sure enough, she showed up at the car at midnight.

On the four-hour drive back I glanced in the rear mirror. Marshall and his friends had fallen asleep but she gave me the finger. Then she started pouring Pepsi onto the floor of my limo. I took a deep breath, then asked her to stop it.

'I'm not doing anything,' she whined. 'See, Marshall, your mom hates me,' she said as she woke up my son.

I drove into a gas station, stopped, opened the rear door and grabbed some paper towels to absorb the liquid on the carpet. Kim just sat there smirking, giving me the finger when my son wasn't looking. When we finally got home Kim came running at me from behind with a footstool. She crashed it over my head, then shouted, 'Come on, Marshall, let's go.' If I hadn't been so relaxed she could've broken my neck.

That was my thanks for twice driving through the night to rescue them when their car had broken down. It wasn't Marshall's fault. But this time I'd really had enough. I banned Kim from our house.

Kim was Marshall's first girlfriend. Before her he was

more interested in creating music in the basement than chasing the opposite sex. I assumed they'd split up eventually but it seemed that the worse she treated him, the more he doted on her. She even mocked his writing.

Marshall carried a notebook everywhere so he could scribble down lyrics. There were piles of them in his bedroom. One evening he stormed into the house, gathered up his books, then threw them into the trash.

'Kim says I'm nothing. I'm a nobody, I'll never make it,' he said.

I pulled the books from the bin and told him not to be stupid. I believed in him, his friends believed in him, he was talented… I told him I never doubted for one minute he would make it.

This scenario was repeated several times over the next few months. Kim knew how to wind him up. It got to the point where I had to use reverse psychology on him.

'OK,' I said, after he'd yet again thrown out his notebooks. 'Kim's right. Her family always said it too. You won't do it. Nobody believes you will. You are useless.'

'No, I'm not,' he said indignantly.

Moments later his notebooks were out of the bin and back in his bedroom.

I knew Marshall had talent. I'd always told him he could achieve anything and, from the moment he announced he was going to be a rapper, I supported him 100 per cent. His lyrics were good. He worked hard at his craft.

No one was prouder than me when he made his stage debut in a talent show at Centerline High School with his pals Mike, Matt and James. Marshall was the front man. He wore white pants and a jacket he'd hand-painted himself with the initials M&M and lots of M&M chocolate sweets. He looked so at home up there on the stage, with his jacket unbuttoned to show off his chest.

James was a pupil at Centerline and their act was good, clean family stuff. They performed for thirty minutes, and the raps were positive. There was nothing about sex, drugs or killing people. I had a Polaroid camera and darted around the stage taking photos. Marshall played to me, making sure I was getting all the right shots.

I never went to any of the Detroit dive clubs where he did his battle MC stuff. He had a hard enough time trying to prove himself without his mom tagging along. He started to work on *Infinite*, his first album. The lyrics I saw – and they were scattered around everywhere on napkins and bits of paper – were all about loving his family and battling with music rivals. There were a few four-letter words but nothing like the crude stuff that came later.

Marshall rarely swore in conversation. He had a fallout with Proof once and I said he had to sort it out.

'I'm fucking trying, Mom,' he snapped.

He said words like that only when he was upset or frustrated. Marshall wasn't brought up around bad language – and although I tried to catch myself many times when Kim provoked me, I was starting to sound like them.

# CHAPTER THIRTEEN

Back in Missouri in the winter of 1991, death descended on my family. Todd shot dead Mike Harris, the crazy guy who'd tried to attack me with a knife when I was pregnant with Nathan. Harris had been stalking Todd, and he threatened to rape and kill his sons. Todd, who'd never had more than a traffic ticket in his life, was now in jail charged with manslaughter. I was preparing to go home to St Joseph to help sort out his defence when my mother called.

She was hysterical, screaming that my youngest brother, nineteen-year-old Ronnie, was dead. I could barely take in what she was saying. All I heard was something about a gun. The police seemed to think it was suicide. I was shaking like a leaf when I put the phone down.

'Ronnie's dead,' I told Marshall.

He shook his head, covered his ears and yelled, 'No, no!' over and over. Then he broke down and cried as I tried to console him.

Ronnie and Marshall were born just two months apart. Technically, they were uncle and nephew but in reality they were more like brothers. They'd grown up together, made a pact to be blood brothers for ever. Ronnie bought Marshall his first album *Reckless* when they were 9 and introduced him to the music of Ice T. They made their first rap demo tapes together.

Ronnie had an unpleasant upbringing. Mom divorced and remarried Ronnie's dad, Ronald Polkingharn, at least twice before marrying her next husband, Carl Coffey before Ronald Snr died. Ronnie was always a gentle soul and we were all surprised when he joined the army. It was probably a way of starting afresh away from the family. But he was discharged almost immediately because he couldn't handle guns. They terrified him. Knowing that made me instantly question the suicide theory.

Marshall felt the same way. He wanted to know who had killed Ronnie. I had my suspicions. I was told by several people that Ronnie had been killed in revenge for Todd's shooting Mike Harris in self-defence.

The next few days were a blur. Marshall refused to come with me to the funeral. He was too upset. I could understand that, so I went alone.

I liaised with the police. As I'd worked at a hospital, it was assumed I could cope better than anyone else. I had to go through the photos of Ronnie's body and the scene. The first thing that struck me was that Ronnie was lying prone, with his finger still on the trigger of the gun.

I tried to get answers about his death. The police said Ronnie and his girlfriend had had a fight. Ronnie broke into a neighbour's house, took a shotgun and fired it. His death was ruled a suicide. It didn't make any sense to me. How could his body be lying in perfect alignment with the gun? I wanted an autopsy but the rest of the family didn't.

Ronnie had an open casket service. He had a white bandage over one eye and a baseball cap pulled over the side of his head. I was devastated and trying to let everything sink in.

Afterwards, once back at the motel where I was staying, Marshall phoned. He was distraught, burbling. I tried to tell him about the service but he didn't want to know.

'Shut the fuck up! Listen to me!' he snapped. 'Remember your living-room set? It's gone, been taken back.'

I couldn't believe what I was hearing. I could hear Kim laughing in the background, goading him to tell me what had happened. Marshall didn't know, and refused to believe that Kim had had my furniture picked up. I had almost finished paying for a beautiful leather sofa and love seat but Kim had phoned the store saying it needed to be picked up because I wouldn't be able to continue to pay for it.

'They came and took it away,' Marshall said.

'Why?' I asked. 'Why did you do this?'

'Fuck you, bitch!' he shouted.

My legs gave way. He swore occasionally but he had never addressed me like that before. I was crying. I couldn't believe what was happening.

'I hate to say this but I'm sick of you,' I screamed. 'I wish this was you instead of Ronnie.'

That comment came out of nowhere. I didn't mean it but I was just so rattled. I'd had to look at pictures of Ronnie dead, kiss his face in the coffin, trying to keep Mom in line while she out of it with grief, and visit Todd in jail. Now Marshall had become abusive. I was under so much pressure because I never knew what Kim was going to do next. I phoned Marshall straight back.

'Son, I am so sorry. I didn't mean it,' I said. He hung up on me.

Now I couldn't stop the tears from falling. It was like a bad dream. I was crying for Ronnie and I was crying for what I had just said to Marshall.

I have apologised to Marshall so many times for saying I wished he was dead instead of Ronnie. *Of course* I didn't mean it. But Marshall refused even to discuss the subject. His feelings came out ten years later on 'Cleanin' Out My Closet' when he used my words against me and said that I was now dead to him. I can't listen to it without sobbing. I am so sorry I said that. It's something I will regret to my dying day.

After Ronnie's death, Marshall fell into a deep depression. He's since said he was struck dumb for three days afterwards and considered killing himself as he listened to the tapes they'd made together. He locked himself away, writing. References to Ronnie are scattered throughout my son's songs, including his chart-topping single 'Stan'. He also part-dedicated *The Marshall Mathers LP* to his memory.

I wrote down my feelings, too. Letters to Marshall, poems penned in the middle of the night when I couldn't sleep for grief. The year after Ronnie died was a dark time for us all.

Todd remained in jail. It took a year for his case to go to trial. We all assumed he'd get off. He killed a crazy guy threatening to rape and murder his kids. Any father would have done the same. I spent hours with Todd and his lawyers going through the evidence.

Mike Harris had been the local nut in their life, and a menace to the police department. He had come at me glassy-eyed with a knife when I was pregnant. Todd had met Janice, the woman who was to become his second wife and the mother of his youngest sons, Korey and Bobby. Mike Harris was her brother.

Harris was insanely jealous of Todd. He shot out the windows of his house, he fired at his white German shepherd dog, he put sugar in the gas tank of the antique truck Todd was restoring, destroying the engine. When Todd took the kids fishing, Harris appeared from nowhere and threw his angling gear into the lake.

Todd did everything to avoid Harris but the man just would not let up. Todd's marriage was in trouble, too.

Janice had become close to my father, Bob Nelson. Who knows what was happening there? But when her second son was born she called him Bobby Ray Nelson in honour of my long-absent dad. Todd told me all this on a visit to Michigan, then he flew back to Missouri.

Janice picked him up at the airport. He was exhausted and hungry and hadn't slept on the flight. Todd had baby Bobby with him and while Janice popped into the grocery store he stayed in the car to mind the baby and three-year-old Korey.

Harris appeared from nowhere, shouting, 'I'm going to rape the little bastard on the back seat.' He tried to yank the car door open. Todd shouted at him to go away. He was rummaging in the glove compartment for the spare car keys when he found an antique gun belonging to Janice. He waved it at Harris, who fled.

A few minutes later, Harris reappeared with a sawn-off shotgun. He shouted, 'I'm going to kill the kids!' He concealed the gun in a paper bag in his ex-wife's car which was blocking Todd in, ran back towards Todd's car and tried to open the door to get to the boys.

Terrified of his motives, Todd cracked. He grabbed the rusty old .38, jumped out of the car and just fired and fired. Harris tried to karate-kick him, spinning around, grunting death threats. A bullet caught him in the back of his shoulder blade.

Janice re-emerged from the store. Todd asked her to drive him to the police station. He walked inside, shocked and pale and nauseous, and handed over the gun.

Ballistics experts said Harris was running away when he was hit by the bullet.

Todd's first lawyer suggested he plead temporary insanity but Todd refused. He knew he was innocent. I agreed. But he was charged with manslaughter and gun possession, and denied bail. Todd rightly insisted on a trial. He was not guilty.

I wasn't allowed inside court because I had a history with Harris. The defence wanted to call me to tell the jury what had happened when I was pregnant with Nathan. I spent the entire two weeks sitting outside the court. In the end I wasn't needed and was allowed inside for the final day. Todd was found guilty and sentenced to eight years – five for manslaughter and three for the gun offence.

It didn't matter how many times I banned Kim from the house, she always returned. She'd flounce through the door, give me the finger and say to Marshall, 'You have a choice – me or your mom.'

Not even Marshall's friends could understand the hold she had over him. I once asked him, 'What is it about her? She can't be that good.'

He just shrugged and said, 'She's my girl, you're my mom. I'm in the middle.'

He said he felt as if he were in the midst of a tug of war. I felt the same, except it was Kim in the middle, pushing Marshall and me apart. She drove me crazy, breaking my ornaments, taking my stuff, calling the protective services. She was horrible to Nathan, too. She simply referred to him as 'the little bastard' – but only when Marshall wasn't in earshot.

When a live tarantula arrived in the mail addressed to me, I called the cops. I was constantly on edge. This wasn't helped by some neighbours' kids who were constantly jumping on Nathan when he'd go out to play.

Nathan, who was six, was friends with some children who lived just up the road on Dresden. They came over crying, saying their mother was drunk and had hurt them. Nathan hung his head. One of the kids said, 'Mama hurt him too.'

I drove over to the woman's house with Marshall and Kim to confront her. She was ex-military, twice my size and walked like a man. She flicked a lit cigarette into my hair. I grabbed hold of her and pinned her against a tree. I was like dynamite. I'd have pummelled her into the ground if Marshall hadn't pulled me off her. Even I couldn't believe I'd floored a military woman twice my size. I'm not violent – I'd never had a fight before – but I'm a tiger when it comes to kids. No one hurts them.

The police questioned us both. I told them what the woman had done. The family split the next day; they just packed up and left. Then someone fire-bombed their house. The detectives quizzed me. I knew nothing about it but it was time to move.

I couldn't sell the house. The area was going downhill; most people were moving out as renters were moving in. I rented it to a couple who seemed nice and put down a deposit on a cute place I'd found in St Clair Shores, 13 miles from downtown Detroit. Until 1951, when it became a city in its own right, it was known as the largest village in the United States. The punk singer Patti Smith raised her family in St Clair, although by the time we moved there it had seen better days.

Marshall got a $5.50-an-hour job at Gilbert's Lodge Restaurant with his old school friend Mike Ruby. When they weren't working, they were making music. Marshall was M&M; Mike called himself Manix. I thought they were great and did my best to keep their spirits up when the Detroit rap scene thought otherwise. Kim didn't help his confidence – she constantly derided him for being 'nothing but a hamburger flipper'.

Not that Kim worked much. She wanted to be a model – she was certainly tall enough – but she didn't seem prepared to work at it. She got jobs here and there, including a brief stint cooking pizzas alongside Marshall at another place, Little Caesars, but they rarely lasted long.

Marshall was still trying to prove himself to Kim's mother and stepfather. But time and again he came home upset because they'd called him 'Mr Smart Ass' and refused to let him in the house.

I did my best to keep his spirits up. I still mothered him, sorting out his car insurance and money problems. When my bills were overdue I kept it to myself – I didn't want him to worry. Even when the couple who rented our old house on Dresden stopped paying, I kept quiet. I struggled to pay for both places and continued to pander to Marshall's needs.

He was always overspending. I blame myself for not teaching him how to balance his bank account. I just didn't want him to worry about such minor things. I lent him money when he needed it and once I cashed his $141.30 paycheque. I gave him $150 in return. Two days later Marshall asked me for his cheque back. He'd spent the money and needed more. I explained I'd cashed it for him. He accused me of stealing it. It didn't matter how many times I explained to him that I'd given him the money already, he could and would not understand it.

'You fucking bitch, you stole my cheque!' he shouted as he stormed out of the house.

Kim followed, saying, 'She took your money,' and uttering other garbage as they left.

That one instance was turned against me in 1999 when he gave interviews saying I ordered him to get a job, took his wages off him and then threw him out of the house. This, he claimed, I did on numerous occasions. I should have defended myself at the time.

Marshall tried living on his own a few times; it was never long before he returned home. Kim found a house in a rough area of Detroit, apparently getting her mom to co-sign. Marshall followed her. It was there that she claimed someone was regularly breaking in and stealing things.

# CHAPTER FOURTEEN

Our house was strangely quiet. I hadn't seen Kim in weeks. Finally, I asked Marshall where she was.

'We've split up,' he said glumly.

I tried not to look too pleased. They were forever breaking up but usually got back together within a few days.

'Do you want to talk about it, son?' I asked.

He shook his head and I decided to leave well alone. A few weeks later he introduced me to Amy, one of the sweetest girls I've ever met. She worked with Marshall at Gilbert's Lodge and appeared to be absolutely smitten with my son.

The moment Kim heard Marshall had a girlfriend she got on the phone. She claimed her new boyfriend had smashed her car windows; she needed Marshall's help.

There was always a drama. Kim called our house constantly. She also rang him at the restaurant. Marshall said she often pretended to be me, conning his co-workers into putting her through.

I thought Marshall had finally seen through Kim, that he was over her and happy with Amy. Then Kim dropped the bombshell that was to change Marshall's life for ever. She was pregnant. My initial reaction was that Marshall couldn't possibly be the father – he hadn't seen Kim in weeks and was happy with Amy. Marshall said he could be the father – it transpired he had been seeing Kim again. He dumped Amy. Chaos reigned once more.

On 17 October 1995, Marshall's twenty-third birthday, Kim brought home a bundle of newborn puppies and let them run loose in the bedroom.

I asked what she was doing with them. She just laughed.

'No, Kim!' I shouted.

But she kept on laughing. I gathered the dogs back up, put them into a cardboard box and ordered her to go to her parents' home to drop off the puppies and then to come back. Marshall was working at Gilbert's Lodge but she phoned him to say she'd been kicked out and forced to go to a rat-infested motel – all untrue. Two hours later Marshall came storming in through the door like a madman.

He started to hit me with his fists. Kim had wound him up with her lies about me throwing her out. As he hit and kicked me over and over, Nathan cowered, crying underneath his blanket. I screamed for mercy, for him to stop.

'Bitch, you want to call 911?' Marshall yelled.

He picked up the phone, dialled the dispatcher and then hung up. Then he really went for me. He grabbed one of the weights he'd been using to bulk up his arm muscles and held it over me.

'Help me God, I will kill you,' he snarled.

At that moment three police officers walked through the door. They'd traced the 911 call. They cuffed him and he was taken off to jail. It was his birthday that day. I begged them only to have him leave, as he needed a cool-down period. He was released the next morning. I refused to press charges, I insisted there wasn't a mark on me. There were plenty, but I could hide them as they were under my clothes.

Now Marshall swears to this day that he cannot remember attacking me. But he had shoved me a few times when he was a teenager, once breaking my finger. He didn't mean to do that; it was an accident. This time he really had hurt me. Yet still I made excuses for him. His blinding temper tantrums started after he was bullied by DeAngelo Bailey. He was like his father; he didn't know what he was doing.

In court, the judge warned Marshall he could get three to five years in jail. I lied when I spoke to the judge. There was no way I was going to lose my son. I told the judge that we'd just buried Ronnie, even though that was almost four years before. I said he was terribly upset over Ronnie's death and that he was under a tremendous amount of stress. I kept on apologising for his behaviour.

Marshall wouldn't look at me. He hung his head when the judge addressed him.

'I'm talking to you,' the judge said. 'You could go away for three to five years. You need to apologise.'

'I'm sorry,' Marshall muttered sullenly.

'Look at your mother,' the judge said.

'I'm sorry, Mom,' Marshall said.

The judge told him he was free to go as long as he agreed to go to counselling. Without my evidence there was no case. Outside court, Marshall and I hugged. I hoped we could put that awful moment behind us.

Once again Kim moved back in with her family. Marshall vowed they were over for good.

The baby was due on my forty-first birthday but Kim went into labour early. She got a friend to phone afterwards.

Marshall grabbed his coat. He couldn't wait to see the baby.

I told him, 'You guys have been broken up for a while. Don't get back with her just because of the baby. Don't let Kim use the baby to soften you up.'

He came home from the hospital several hours later with a massive grin on his face.

'That's my baby,' he said. 'She looks just like me, Mom.'

Kim refused to put his name on the birth certificate. She said it was because she didn't have a father's name on *her* certificate when she was born 20 years earlier, so

118

why should Hailie? It seemed cruel and made no sense, but that was Kim all over.

Marshall was so upset he called the courthouse to try to get his name added. It broke my heart hearing him getting more angry by the minute.

'Look, I'm going to pay child support. I'm her father, I'm bringing up this child,' I heard him shout down the phone.

I took the phone off him and tried to explain to the court official that he wanted to be a responsible parent. The official just said it was up to the mother whether she named the father.

Like Marshall, I too fell in love with Hailie the moment I saw her. It was impossible not to. She was so beautiful and just like my son. And I had no qualms about being a young, glamorous granny!

Needless to say, motherhood did not mellow Kim. She got worse. Now she used Hailie to goad Marshall and me, threatening constantly to stop us seeing her. Marshall would go to get Hailie and many times the police would be called on him, or he'd be told he couldn't see her but just as he was driving away he'd be told he could after all.

But Marshall still wasn't allowed across the threshold of her parents' home, and many times I would drive over to pick Hailie up for him. Kim's twin sister Dawn had a two-year-old daughter, Alaina, whom Marshall also doted on. He wanted to be a father figure to both of them, but Kim's family just laughed at him.

Marshall was determined to prove himself. He started putting in more than 40 hours a week at Gilbert's Lodge. Every penny he earned went on Kim and the baby. When he wasn't working, he was changing Hailie's diapers, playing with her or singing her to sleep, and working on lyrics.

Kim surprised everyone by getting a job as a receptionist in a health spa. Except, as is often the way with Kim, the job wasn't quite what she said it was. She'd once again refused to let Marshall see Hailie. He begged me to try reasoning with her. He stayed in the car while Nathan and I went inside. It didn't look like the sort of health spas I knew. There was a menu of services available. Manicures, pedicures and facials were not on the list.

Marshall suspected she was seeing a guy who ran the spa. She was always out in clubs, drinking and doing God only knows what. Yet still he stood by her. I encouraged him to get back with Amy from Gilbert's Lodge but I think she was too nice for him. He was used to being abused by Kim.

While the chaos between Kim and Marshall remained, I continued to care for Hailie off and on. She was the sweetest little thing and I spoiled her rotten. No one was prouder than I was of being a grandmother.

# CHAPTER FIFTEEN

The 3rd of February 1996 was Nathan's tenth birthday. Three days later he started at a new school. I kissed him goodbye with great trepidation. Just like Marshall at the same age, Nate was being bullied.

He'd been in class just twenty minutes when the social workers swooped in and took him away. They took him off to a youth home and I was charged with an array of offences, including Munchausen syndrome by proxy. I didn't know what that was then, but I'll explain it very shortly. It was every mother's nightmare.

Four months earlier, Nathan had come home from school at 3 p.m. with a large gash on the back of his head. He'd been beaten up at the bus stop at 7 a.m. by two cousins. They'd got into a disagreement about the O J Simpson murder verdict. The footballer had been cleared of killing his wife Nicole and her friend Ron Goldman but, like many people, I thought he was guilty. When the cousins asked Nathan what he thought, he'd parroted my comments. They proceeded to beat him over the head with their fists and a computer keyring, throwing him down onto the pavement before his bus arrived. Nate got up and boarded the bus, and at school he tried to tell staff. He was put in a computer room and ice was applied to the back of his head where he was hurt. He was given a sandwich at lunchtime and then sent home by bus.

Nathan begged me not to send him back to school. It wasn't just the kids who were picking on him: the teachers didn't like him either. He has a form of dyslexia – the educational specialists said he sees words backwards – and he was put in a special-education class. The teachers sat him at the very front, facing the blackboard with his back to the other kids. When Nate complained that he was being hit by stuff thrown from behind, or prodded with sharp pencils while the teacher wasn't looking, he would be put in the corner with a dunce's hat on.

To add to his problems, a few months earlier we were on our way back from Missouri when Nathan tripped on a motel carpet and knocked himself out. He crashed down so hard that one of his teeth fell out. He was rushed to hospital by ambulance and treated for concussion. But the effects were lasting. He was suffering memory lapses and the teachers said he was no longer reading properly. At the request of the school he was placed in a special education class, and was diagnosed with post-concussion syndrome and post-traumatic stress disorder.

Now, bearing in mind that Marshall's doctors wanted him institutionalised after DeAngelo Bailey had attacked him, I was overprotective with Nathan. I'd almost lost one son, so I watched Nathan like a hawk. After the O J Simpson beating, I took him to our doctor who gave me a note to keep Nathan home until he'd recovered.

Nathan begged me not to send him back to that school. I agreed. St Clair Shores was now really rough. I wanted to get him out of the education district. I found a cute little place to buy in Casco Township and rented a temporary apartment nearby while I waited for the mortgage to come through. I told Marshall that he, Kim and Hailie could have the St Clair Shores place as long as they promised to pay the bills. They moved in once the drama with Nathan's school was over.

Then Nathan's school accused me of truancy. I was given a court date in January, only to have it postponed the three times I went to court. The judge advised me to return with a lawyer. Meantime a social worker knocked on my door. I had called protective services' attention to the abuse I felt Nathan was experiencing from kids at his school, but it fell back on me when the kids refused to admit to hurting my son. At first I was relieved to see her though later I would come to regret that feeling. She checked over the house, noting it was clean and full of food. It didn't matter that I had a doctor's note for Nathan: the school wanted him back in class.

I decided maybe we needed to move out of the state. I sent Nate ahead to Missouri, and got my sister Tanya to enrol him in school there while I waited in Michigan for the truancy hearing in January. Sadly my case kept being adjourned and I would have to go and pick up my son.

I spoke to Nathan four times a day and he begged me to come home. He'd never even gone to sleepovers at friends' houses, let alone been parted from me for weeks on end. So I drove back to Missouri to collect him. My family refused to let him leave, so I called the police. It wasn't a big deal, just par for the course with my family. After a cursory check, the officers let Nathan and me go on our way.

We arrived home in the early hours of the morning and barely had a chance to unpack before it was time for him to go to school. It was just after his birthday and he really didn't want to go but I said he'd soon make new friends.

After I'd dropped him off I had a weird feeling that something was wrong, so I called just to double-check. I used the excuse of asking if he had his lunch money. The phone was passed to a child-protective services official, the same one who had visited our house. She told me that Nathan had been taken into state custody and I had to be in court in thirty minutes. They even sent a policeman to my house to make sure I went.

Once at court, I met a long-time friend of mine, Pat,

and her son there, and the officials allowed her into the room with me. It was packed with people. Some were squashed around a big circular table, while others lined the walls.

I kept asking, 'Where's my son?' But the court official ordered me to be quiet.

As the charges were read out I wanted to scream. I was accused of keeping Nathan away from school; that I had struck him with a belt or hairbrush; and that once I had chased him out of the house for listening to rap music.

I'd never raised a finger to Nathan and he grew up listening to Marshall's rap music. In shock, I stated that the charges were all lies. Again, I was told to shut up.

Then came the oddest charge: I was suffering from Munchausen by proxy. I looked at Betsy Mellos, my lawyer, to see if she knew what that was. She shrugged. I'm tiny, and so was Nathan's father. I guess I was thinking of the Munchkins in *The Wizard of Oz* – that our genes had also made Nathan small for his age at the time. It had to be some form of dwarfism, I thought.

The case was adjourned. I begged that I wanted to be with my son but the case workers refused to tell me where he was. I was only told I was to go next door and sign some papers in case of Nathan ever needing medical treatment while away from me. I wondered how bizarre this situation was.

Betsy and I sat in her office for hours going through the paperwork, trying to decide what to do next. We also looked up Munchausen by proxy. It did not make for pleasant reading. Munchausen syndrome itself is a psychological disorder. Sufferers deliberately harm themselves for attention. Munchausen *by proxy* is rare and far more serious. It is one of the most harmful forms of child abuse. Sufferers are usually female and have probably been abused themselves as kids.

I shook as I read the diagnosis. It said the mainly female sufferers exaggerated, fabricated and even induced illnesses, often fooling doctors into carrying out unnecessary tests and surgery on the child. There were instances of mothers scrubbing a child with cleaning fluids to create rashes or deliberately reopening wounds so they would not heal. It was said sufferers wanted attention from doctors.

A British doctor, Sir Richard Asher, father of the actress Jane, named the self-harming disease in 1951 after the seventeenth-century pathological liar, Baron von Munchausen. In 1977 the British paediatrician Sir Roy Meadow added the words 'by proxy' to include parents who hurt – and even killed – their children.

'I've never hurt a child,' I sobbed to Betsy. 'The school's just saying this because they've been abusing Nathan.' Betsy was so sweet and supportive. She had twins herself and knew I would never hurt my son.

I knew the Munchausen-by-proxy charge was a trumped-up one – an easy way of taking Nathan away into foster care – but I had to prove it.

After I left the court building I went into the youth home to sign the papers. As I started to sign, I ripped through the paperwork when making a large X on it; I was screaming for Nathan. The staff refused to let me see him. I ran out of there, in shock. My friend Pat, who'd been with me throughout the day, and her son yanked me into their car.

Pat had just lost her husband. In the court room, as the charges were being read, she had said, 'I thought my husband dying after fifty years of marriage was bad, but it's nothing compared with this.' She was told to keep quiet.

On the way back I couldn't even talk for sobbing. Back at the house it was even worse. Nathan's bike was propped up in the kitchen. His toys were on the floor. I could only imagine what he was going through. He'd be trying to sleep in some stranger's house or the jail-like youth home. I couldn't even phone him. I had no idea where he was. Questions kept filling my head: was he really at a youth home? Did he know I was trying to help him? Dear God, how could they do this to me and my son? I thought I was on the verge of a breakdown. I hoped and prayed for my son to come home. So did he.

The next month went past in a blur. I continued working, studying at pharmacy tech school and looking after Hailie whenever I could. She was blossoming into a beautiful little girl, but my heart ached for Nathan. Finally, it was agreed I could have a supervised visit at a youth home.

It was freezing cold but Nathan was dressed in short-sleeved pyjamas. I'd been warned I couldn't hug him but I reached out to touch his arm. A social worker shouted at me. He was blue with cold. I couldn't stop crying. Nathan begged me over and over to take him home. It was heartbreaking. I had to explain to him that the authorities wouldn't even tell me where he was living.

A few days later I received a letter saying I could not see Nathan again. Betsy and I fought for two weeks until I was allowed another supervised visit. It wasn't any easier but at least I saw him.

For the next four months I was allowed to visit every other week, then once a week and finally I was allowed to see him alone. We sat in a little cubicle, surrounded by other parents and kids in identical cubicles. Several social workers stood nearby listening to everything we said. They hovered menacingly every time Nathan tried to tell me about his foster parents being cruel to him. He drew pictures of himself and wrote the word *help* in speech bubbles. I knew I had to get him away from foster care, whatever it took.

Nathan's father was asked if he wanted to see his son. I ran into him in the parking lot and he asked me if I'd sever his rights to Nathan. I couldn't believe it. How dare he say that? I would have run him over if I could have got away with it. I told him no, and to leave us alone. I asked the assigned social worker to please allow Marshall to see Nathan in place of Nate's dad. She talked to Marshall and finally agreed.

So Marshall was allowed visits. Now he was almost

twenty-four and a father himself. He was busy himself but he felt obliged to spend time with his little brother.

I had a hunch: I'd read somewhere that Native American children weren't allowed to be taken into foster care. They had to go to extended-family members. Through my father's family, I was part Cherokee. I'd grown up hearing stories from Nan about our famous ancestor Betsy Webb on the Trail of Tears. I went to the library and also made several phone calls to investigate further. Sure enough, I found the proof I needed.

The Indian Child Welfare Act of 1978 was designed to stop Native American families being broken up and adopted by non-Indians. The law decreed that if a child was a tribe member or eligible for membership they could not just be taken away into foster care. The child had to be placed with relatives or tribe leaders.

The protective-services people were indignant. Nathan has dark eyes and an olive complexion, but I'm fair with blue eyes.

'Oh, bullshit, you're no American Indian,' one case worker said. I just smiled.

With Nan's help I tracked our history back to the Echota Tribe of Alabama. Then I called the tribe. They couldn't have been more helpful. We did lots of research and, sure enough, we were eligible. Nathan and I were issued with tribal membership cards. Marshall said he didn't want one – he preferred to hang onto his Scottish heritage. He also believed he was part Irish because my half-sister Betti Renee's father, Ron Gilpin, was. It didn't matter how many times I told him that wasn't the case, he insisted on celebrating St Patrick's Day.

I was fascinated by the history of the Echota Cherokee. They'd lived peacefully alongside the first English settlers but by the end of the seventeenth century had been forced into war over land. In 1838 during federal removal they'd been ordered to join the Trail of Tears to Oklahoma. But a handful managed to remain, living secretly, denying their heritage. In the 1910 US census, just nine Cherokees were listed as living in Alabama; today there are 22,000. The tribe was not officially recognised until 1980, and then only recognised in state but not federal law. The name Echota was chosen because the word means sanctuary. It was something the tribe now offered Nathan and me. If the court wouldn't let me have Nathan back, the tribe would take Nathan. We had a safe haven: all we had to do now was prove it in court. And thank God that the American Indian Association and Faye Gibbons encouraged me to fight on.

# CHAPTER SIXTEEN

M arshall and I agreed that Christmas 1996 was the lowest point for our family. Nathan was still in foster care and I was trying desperately to get him back. Kim and Marshall stayed at my house in St Clair Shores, while I moved to the new place in Casco Township where there were better schools for Nathan. My lawyer suggested I stay away from Marshall otherwise he too could lose his visitation rights to Nathan. We weren't to speak to each other, even when he brought Nate to the house in St Clair Shores on the couple of times they allowed Nate to stay the day or overnight there.

I remember going by there just to watch through the front window as Nate sat on the floor playing with Hailie. My heart was broken. I felt I should be in there with them. Marshall once caught me, and told me I had to leave or he'd lose his visits with Nathan. I was shattered. I cried all the way home.

Then Marshall lost his job at Gilbert's Lodge and his debut solo album *Infinite* flopped. He reckoned he'd sold maybe 500 copies and the only mentions he got on local radio were mocking. The disc jockeys said he was a phoney just like Vanilla Ice. They even laughed at him for thanking Kim and me for our support.

I loved *Infinite* and felt so proud of Marshall. He'd written about his struggles to support Hailie, his feelings for Kim and his rap battles at the Hip-Hop Shop, where he now had a regular Saturday-night gig.

He got one positive review. *Underground Soundz* noted, 'His mastery of the English language allows him to write coherent stories, not just freestyle ramblings that happen to rhyme.'

I tried to cheer him up, saying he'd proved his teachers wrong when they'd given him C grades in English. But Marshall just shook his head in despair. One of the tracks, 'Searchin'', got occasional airplay in Detroit, but he knew it wasn't enough to gain national attention. He kept on writing but he no longer showed me his lyrics.

Marshall was subpoenaed by the state of Michigan to testify against me. He had no choice in the matter but was deeply unhappy about it.

The trial date was set for 15 April. I was charged with neglect and abuse of Nathan. My lawyers Betsy Mellos and Mike Friedman were working with the Macomb

County prosecutors on a possible plea bargain, but I wanted a jury trial. I wasn't going to leave anything to chance. Almost 150 people, including medical experts for both sides, had been called to give evidence. I had seen three psychiatrists, enrolled in good-parenting classes and enlisted the help of our local media. The headline in the *Macomb Daily* on the day of the trial read, MOTHER ACCUSED OF HARMING HER CHILD FOR SYMPATHY. It went on to explain Munchausen syndrome by proxy.

Marshall was one of the first witnesses to take the stand for the prosecution. The court officials sniggered at his big baggy pants. They pulled faces behind his back.

The state lawyers asked him about our house in St Clair Shores, where he was still living with Kim. They hadn't paid the bills, and the house was being foreclosed. The lawyers tried to make Marshall look like an ass because he didn't understand the difference between cancelled cheques, which had been paid, and duplicate ones, which were merely copies.

Then he tried to explain how he thought Nathan might have drunk from a baby bottle until he was 6 or 7. The lawyer asked, 'So did he take it to school with him?' Many people chuckled as Marshall said 'No'. He pointed out that Nathan had always been fed proper food.

When asked if I was a good or bad mother, Marshall didn't hesitate in answering, 'She's a good mom.'

He also said I'd never hurt Nathan, that I had never done anything wrong beyond maybe striking Nate on his rear end once when he was a five-year-old. For a witness called by the opposition, he'd done a great job for my defence.

They also asked him, 'Do you love your mother?' He did not reply.

Other witnesses were called. The school claimed I'd taken Nathan to nine or ten different doctors. I could prove otherwise. Our lovely long-time family GP Dr Sal said that wasn't the case. He made me – and the judge – smile when asked what sort of a mother I was, and referred to Joan Clever, the perfect mom in the popular American TV series *Leave It to Beaver*.

'She may not be Joan Clever but she's awfully damn close,' he said.

Nathan had been to the doctor eight times in nine years. I worried that the judge would say that wasn't enough. Also, in the sixteen months he'd been in foster care, he'd had numerous accidents and needed medical treatment after breaking several fingers and hurting his collarbone. He'd also been badly hurt when someone hit him in the eye with a golf club.

Three days into the trial, the case abruptly stopped. My lawyers and the prosecution had reached a plea bargain. If I agreed to cooperate fully with social workers visiting our house, take parenting classes and give an assurance that Nathan would go to school, I could have him back. Nathan begged me to agree and, of course, I said yes.

We still had to wait a few more weeks before Nathan was finally allowed home. He had to finish school first. I organised a big welcome-back party, decking up the house with balloons and ribbons. All the neighbours and their children came along. The local newspaper took a beautiful photo of us being reunited.

I'd worked very closely with the American Indian Association. One of the staff, Faye Gibbons, had become a friend. She always remarked on my fighting sprit.

'You're not a survivor: you're an overachiever,' she said. 'Even that's an understatement. If there were four of you, you'd be running the country.'

I told her I was going to fight on, using the Indian Child Welfare Act to make sure no other Native American would be removed from a family member. She encouraged me totally and was as delighted as I was when Michigan's Children's Ombudsman ruled Macomb County hadn't complied with state law or Family Independence Agency policy when they removed Nathan. The letter said that the FIA was now working with tribal members to revise and update their policies. I'd set a precedent; I knew it would help countless families in the future.

Meanwhile, Marshall was going through another off episode with Kim. He moved in with us – Nan was living with us too. Marshall was allowed to have Hailie stay, sometimes for days at a time. I was thrilled. Hailie was such a bright little thing. Every evening after she'd brushed her hair, she'd spin around in a nightdress in front of the mirror and ask, 'Am I beautiful?' We'd all chorus back that she was. I nicknamed her Fuss Bucket; she called me Mama.

'Don't ever let Kim hear her call you Mama,' Marshall warned. I agreed. Kim still flitted in and out of our lives, creating havoc.

Marshall got a mention in *The Source* magazine's 'Unsigned Hype' column. The skinny white kid had conquered his critics on the Detroit music scene and now he was one of their star freestyle rappers. The radio station disc jockeys who had once laughed at him now invited him to perform on air.

He'd also created a new alter ego: Slim Shady was a comic antihero who inflicted violence on all the people who'd annoyed Marshall in the past. This, he told me, included school bullies, Kim and the people who'd sneered at his *Infinite* album.

'It's a big joke, Mom,' he assured me. 'The songs are funny. They aren't meant to be taken seriously.'

Detroit producers Mark and Jeff Bass had believed in Marshall when no one else did. He'd recorded *Infinite* in their studio and at the beginning of 1997 he was back there again recording *The Slim Shady EP*.

Suddenly there was a buzz about Marshall, or should I say Eminem and Slim Shady? He was still flat broke, struggling to support Hailie and battling constantly with Kim. But on the Detroit rap scene he was famous.

He flew to Los Angeles to take part in the Rap Olympics, where he came second out of fifty contestants. He performed live on an influential radio programme called *The Wake-Up Show*. Not long afterwards he was named as

*The Wake-Up Show*'s freestyle performer of the year. Along the way, Marshall caught the attention of Dr Dre.

He came back from LA all excited, talking nonstop. I took a phone call from Dre. As I handed the phone to Marshall, he high-fived me, covered the receiver with one hand, then punched the air mouthing, 'Yes, yes!'

Dre helped form NWA – originally known as Niggaz With Attitude – in the late 1980s. Their album *Straight Outta Compton* was one of Marshall's favourites. At seventeen he'd wanted to be Dre – lip-synching in sunglasses in front of the bedroom mirror! Dre quit NWA to produce for Death Row Records. When he left to start his own label Aftermath, I predicted he'd be a perfect match for Marshall. Dre was keen to discover unsigned new acts.

Now, finally, Marshall was getting the big break I knew he deserved after years of rejection. In January 1998 he signed with Aftermath and went straight into Dre's Los Angeles recording studio. He phoned to talk to me, Hailie and Nate every other night. He knew that when Hailie was there she was in good hands – we had so much fun, going to Chuck E Cheese's, Fun House Pizza and bumper-bowling.

Marshall was full of excitement, telling me about the people he'd met, the lyrics he'd recorded and his plans for a national tour. He finished every conversation, as he always did, by telling me he loved me and that he couldn't wait to get back to see his baby girl, Nan and the rest of us.

When Marshall returned home almost a month later his language was foul and he'd invented another new persona for himself. He said he had to prove himself to the hip-hop industry because of his colour. He was constantly fighting against prejudice from people who wrongly assumed that he was rich and born with a silver spoon in his mouth.

I found fifteen to twenty pills on his bedroom floor. He told me they were aspirin. I was worried Hailie or the dog would swallow them, so I flushed them down the toilet. He went berserk when he woke up. The pills were Vicodin, really strong painkillers.

He'd had problems sleeping; now he said the pills helped.

Kim was back on the scene again. Marshall was no longer 'a useless nobody', as she called him. He was on his way to becoming a rap star. She was now a looming presence at his concerts; she loved the fame and glamour. I was told she also fed him pills to calm his stage fright.

When Marshall wasn't on the road, he was rapping in Detroit. But he didn't forget his old friends. I still have a hand-drawn poster he did for an outdoor concert, featuring Proof, Da Klinic and Mass Hysteria, on 25 July 1998.

He didn't play me any of his Slim Shady songs. But as far as I knew they weren't offensive – he needed radio airplay. The lyric sheets he left lying around usually mentioned Hailie, although one dealt with a pill overdose, noting he was 'scared of losin' everything I got'.

He was almost 26, still living at home and the thing he feared losing most of all was his daughter.

After years of being alone I'd fallen in love again. John Briggs was about to become husband number four. Everyone loved John, except Marshall.

When I tried to introduce them, Marshall said, 'Keep that son of a bitch away from me.'

He was furious when John and I decided to make a fresh start in St Joseph.

'If you leave you'll miss out on Hailie,' he said.

I told him not to be silly, that I'd be back to visit all the time.

'You'll regret it. I'll never speak to you again if you go back to St Joe,' he said.

'Why? What's the problem?' I asked.

'You can forget about me,' he warned. 'I don't like the creep.'

Marshall wanted me to stay in Casco Township. He loved the area the house was in, and was very comfortable with all of us there – it was very nice.

I talked to Nan, who was in ailing health. She encouraged me to move. Nan would come to Missouri in a few months. Meanwhile, she wanted to go back to her home in Warren, where Todd was living. Nathan also was happier in Missouri. I tried to explain all this to Marshall but he still wasn't happy.

'Son, you have your life now,' I said. 'You have Hailie and Kim. Your career is about to take off. Please let me have a life too.'

'You have a life here with me, Nathan, Hailie and Nan,' he said.

In the end we agreed that he could keep the house – once again Kim promised to pay the bills and make the mortgage repayments. I left all the utilities in my name and started making preparations to move back to St Joe.

# CHAPTER SEVENTEEN

I was crazy about John Briggs. He was tall, just like Marshall's father Bruce, two years younger than me and incredibly handsome. I was leery about marrying again but I'd been on my own for so long and I loved his company.

He'd been married twice before – and was still friends with his last ex-wife. Nan and Nathan really liked John; even our dog liked him.

We bought a house together in St Joe. It was a cute two-bedroom cottage with a good half-acre of land at the back. I wanted to wait a while before we married but John was keen to tie the knot sooner rather than later.

It was just before Thanksgiving and Sharon Spiegel, the minister at the South Park Christian Academy and Church, where my brother Ronnie had gone to school, agreed to officiate.

The ceremony was at Sharon's home with just my sister Tanya, my mother and her latest husband Dutch in attendance. It was very low-key although I did splash out on a long, blue, sleeveless gown. I'd always used the name Mathers for Marshall's sake, but John wanted me to take his surname. We compromised, and I became Mrs Mathers-Briggs.

Soon my limo service took off in St Joseph. I knew the business from my previous company years before in Michigan. I purchased a Lincoln limo and started a new company. I had previously met Bill Hill, an old friend who ran a cab company and for whom my aunt worked, so I also helped out as a dispatcher for him. I introduced him to Kim and Marshall, and he catered to their every need, driving them wherever they pleased, and refusing to take even a dime from my son. It was spoiled by someone in my family who fed some lies to Bill's parole officer, causing him to be pulled up for a parole violation. When he was briefly sent to jail I kept the business running as long as I could for him. He was so lovely to my son and everyone.

John, who hadn't worked while married to his second wife, got a job in construction. But he hated doing manual work and he resented the fact that I made more money than he did. He started drinking heavily. He could go through one or two cases of beer – up to twenty-four bottles – in a day. When I asked him why, he said he was homesick and missed his friends in Michigan. He also admitted that he'd drunk like that for most of his adult life. Then, when I was in hospital for surgery, Nathan called to say he was alone – John had taken off.

Nathan and I drove back to Michigan to spend Christmas with Marshall, Kim and Hailie. We hadn't been in the house two hours when John came knocking on the door.

'You want me to tell him to leave?' Marshall shouted.

'That's my wife,' said John.

'I don't give a damn. Leave!' Marshall snarled.

John begged to talk to me, and I hoped we could work things out. But Marshall refused to let him into the house.

John and I drove to a motel so we could discuss our future. I tried calling Marshall but he snapped, 'You made your choice. You chose John over me.'

Then – *click* – the phone went dead. Every time I tried to call, he cut me off. Marshall often said he felt he was in the middle of a tug of war between Kim and me. Now I felt caught between Marshall and John.

We drove back to Missouri with John promising he really had given up drinking. We'd missed each other so much and, alcohol aside, got on so well. We never argued. But within weeks he was sullen, once more resentful about having to do manual work. Then he started drinking again.

I felt as if I were going to hell in a hand basket. Why had I been so stupid? Just like my mother, I attracted drunks.

At the beginning of February John took off again. He just disappeared. My fourth marriage had gone the way of my previous three.

There was little point in moving back to Michigan. Anyway, Nathan preferred St Joseph. Marshall still telephoned every other night. If he wasn't on the road doing concerts, he was in the studio recording. *The Slim Shady LP* was slated for release on 23 February 1999. Marshall said the first single, 'Just Don't Give a Fuck', and 'Brain Damage' would go out a few weeks earlier. He was also excited by his press coverage: he was forever telling me to go out and buy *Spin*, *The Source*, *Vibe* and whatever. He also excited because *Rolling Stone* was putting him on the cover.

I was so proud of my son. I'd never doubted his talent, I always knew he'd make it. But even I was stunned at the speed he became an overnight sensation. Nathan had the television tuned to MTV – Marshall was on constantly. He called to say the single was in the Top 10. 'My Name Is' followed and *The Slim Shady LP* entered the Billboard pop chart at Number 2. Eminem was the name on everyone's lips. My son Marshall was a star.

When *The Slim Shady LP* also topped the R&B charts, he was compared to Elvis Presley. Almost fifty years earlier, Elvis had taken traditional black music from the South and turned it mainstream. Now my son was doing the same thing with rap.

I heard the radio versions of his songs and watched his videos on TV. I had no idea how filthy his real lyrics were.

When Anthony Bozza from *Rolling Stone* phoned me, I was happy to give an interview. He'd been on tour with

Marshall and told me I must be proud of him. We exchanged a few pleasantries, then Bozza asked me how I felt about being called 'a fucking bitch' by Marshall.

I was so shocked I can't even remember how I replied. But I know I let slip Marshall's real age. He hadn't warned me he'd shaved two years off his birth date to appear much younger.

When the article appeared at the end of April my phone started ringing off the hook. It was full of lies.

Marshall, pictured naked with an exploding stick of dynamite covering his manhood, had invented a new mother. Apparently I was a drunk, 'pill-popping, lawsuit-happy mom'. At fifteen, I'd ordered him to get a job, then constantly kicked him out after taking his wages off him.

I phoned Marshall in tears and begged to know why he'd said those things.

'It's nothing,' he said. That was it. He refused to discuss it any further.

Other magazines copied Marshall's quotes in *Rolling Stone*. It's one of the most prestigious magazines in the world, a gospel for music lovers, so no one doubted the interview. Every day there appeared to be a nastier, more lurid story in the media. Then Marshall gave MTV a tour of the house in Casco Township. He gave the impression it was his but he was about to abandon it for a big mansion.

I received letters from the finance company saying the payments had not been made.

'We don't want your fucking place,' Kim said, when I phoned to find out what was happening.

Marshall assured me it was just a misunderstanding. Kim had missed just one payment while he was on tour. It had all been sorted out. Anyway, he said, he was now flush with money. Soon he'd be able to buy a new house. His album had sold two million copies just in America. He was also Number 1 in the United Kingdom and numerous other places across the world.

As always at the end of our conversations, he told me he loved and missed me. But this time he added excitedly that he was going to see me really soon. He was doing a show in Lawrence, Kansas, three hours' drive from St Joseph and he wanted me there. Of course, I said yes. The only time I'd ever seen him perform was at the Centerline School talent show almost ten years earlier.

It still hadn't hit me that my son Marshall was now Eminem, the hottest rap act going. Word soon got out in St Joseph that he was a local lad made good. Teenagers knocked on my door – they wanted *my* autograph! Nathan was bombarded with kids wanting signed posters. It seemed as if everywhere we went, everyone knew who we were.

I made the front page of the *St Joseph News-Press*. The headline read RAPPER EMINEM JUST REGULAR SON TO MOM. I was described as his number-one fan and quoted as saying, 'I don't think of him as anyone other than Marshall.' I admitted being 'very heartbroken' by his comments in *Rolling Stone* but explained that the persona of Eminem was nothing like the private Marshall.

It was a really nice article – nothing like the usual stories that accused Marshall of being a profanity-spewing, drug-taking, violent misogynist. I told the reporter Linda Wiedmaier I'd meet her at Liberty Hall, where the concert was taking place, so she could hang out with us.

Nathan couldn't wait to see his brother. As we arrived at the venue there were literally hundreds of fans milling around. The roads were blocked off. I worried that the crowd would get out of control.

Nathan was so excited – we were all backstage, and Marshall wanted him out on the stage at the end of the set. I wasn't sure, and nervously I watched to make sure Nate didn't get grabbed. We were whisked around the back to Marshall's tour bus. He was delighted to see us but looked exhausted.

We sat on the bus until it was time for him to go on stage. There were all sorts of people milling around him, including Tanya and Betti Renee, her husband Jack and various other family members. Marshall kept swigging from a water bottle. I later discovered it was full of Bacardi.

As I got off the bus I was stopped by a boy of about eight who'd been hanging around in the rain.

'Ma'am, are you his mother?' he asked.

'Sure am,' I said.

'I've been trying to get his autograph for four hours,' he said. 'It's raining. Do you think you can get me one?'

He told me his brother was suffering from leukaemia.

I said I'd see what I could do, but as I tried to get back onto the bus I was stopped by a bodyguard. I told him about the little boy, explaining he had an Eminem baseball cap he'd like signing.

The guard just shook his head and said, 'No. He's done enough autographs for the night.'

I felt so sad for the boy, so I signed the cap instead. Then I slipped inside Liberty Hall for the start of the concert.

Marshall played for thirty-five minutes. I bobbed around taking photographs. Nathan darted from the wings and fired a power water pump at the audience during the finale. My heart was in my mouth: I feared the crowd would surge forward and grab Nathan. Then, in a flash, the lights went down and Marshall was gone. He'd explained earlier that he'd be on the bus and en route to the next city before the fans knew he'd left the building.

I retrieved Nathan backstage and then we wandered outside. Still there were fans milling around. When word went out that I was Marshall's mom, I was mobbed. I must have signed a dozen autographs.

The next day's *St Joseph News-Press* carried an article headlined HANGING OUT WITH EMINEM'S MOM. The reporter, Linda, wrote a really sweet article describing my 'pretty, fragile features' and long blonde hair.

If not for the hair, eyes and chic hippie-chick outfit of gold embroidered pants and vest over a black body suit, she might not have been noticed among her son's young fans. Most of the teens and twenty somethings were larger than the '5ft 2 and 98 pounds dripping wet' Debbie. But none were probably as formidable.

The article went on to describe how I'd raised my two sons almost single-handedly, that I'd fostered other children, worked for Mothers Against Drunk Drivers, was a Make-A-Wish volunteer, had taught myself to talk again after the 1991 car crash and now ran my own limousine service.

I was delighted. Someone had finally set the record straight. Now I hoped all the horrible magazine writers and rap fans would read that and realise I wasn't a pill-popping, pot-smoking, alcoholic crazy woman.

I was nothing if not naïve.

# CHAPTER EIGHTEEN

It's traditional for the bride's mother to shed a few tears at her daughter's wedding. But, when my son Marshall married Kim, I cried throughout the entire 30-minute ceremony. It was the saddest day of my life.

I know I should have been pleased, if only for my granddaughter Hailie's sake. Marshall had begged for my blessing.

'Mom, I love her. We've been together all this time. We have a child together. Be happy for us, please,' he'd said. I didn't have the heart to tell him about the vile faces Kim pulled behind his back after they'd told me they were getting married.

The proposal hadn't exactly come out of the blue. After all, they'd been together since Kim was thirteen and Marshall was fifteen. He was now twenty-six, and a doting dad himself; he kept telling me he knew his own mind. But, until a few months before, he'd been a nobody – as Kim constantly reminded him. Now the former $5.50 an hour hamburger flipper was Eminem, the international superstar. I did wonder about Kim's motives.

A few days earlier, Marshall took a break from touring to drive into St Joseph for my sister Tanya's wedding. Hailie was three and a half and supposed to be a flower girl. But she'd bowed out at the last minute, refusing to walk down the aisle. Afterwards, she was upset for missing out. Somehow, Marshall had suggested a second wedding to please her.

They came rushing into my house to tell me this. Marshall had the biggest grin on his face. He leaned forward to hug Kim. She's six foot, a good few inches taller than he is. As she leaned over his shoulder, she stared me in the eye, pretended to put her fingers down her throat and pretended to vomit.

I tried to ignore her as she purred, 'We don't need a prenup. I'm not marrying you for your money, Marshall. I love you.'

It was a very sick joke. She caught my eye again, then made more puking gestures with her fingers.

Moments later she was on the phone to her own mother, barking orders about buying a house. Marshall was out the back with Nate and Hailie and didn't hear her make the call. When he came back in he tugged at her sleeve. They were keen to get to the city hall to collect a marriage licence.

I tried to delay them. There was no reason to marry so suddenly. But Kim insisted they wanted to tie the knot there and then in the town where he'd been born. They took off for the city hall, a twenty-minute drive away. It was 4.45 p.m. and the building closed at five o'clock. With luck, they'd find the doors locked. But I didn't want to take that chance. I phoned and begged them not to let them in.

Marshall and Kim returned an hour or so later, full of smiles. They'd arrived at 5.10 p.m. Apparently, the building stayed open late specially because Marshall was now such a big star.

Looking back, I'm amazed word didn't leak out there and then about the celebrity wedding. After all, St Joseph isn't exactly big on stars. It's known as the birthplace of the Hollywood actress and one-time Mrs Ronald Reagan, Jane Wyman, the home of the Pony Express and the town where the outlaw Jesse James died.

I tried a different tack. Marshall wanted a tiny wedding, with just me and our taxi owner friend Bill Hill as witnesses. I asked him to at least let his manager, Paul Rosenberg, know about it. I was pretty sure Paul would put a stop to the wedding. But Marshall refused to call him.

That night when Kim popped out to the shops, I begged Marshall not to marry her. I couldn't tell him that Kim had made vomiting gestures behind his back, but I wanted him to know I didn't approve. They'd been breaking up and making up for almost twelve years.

Kim's parents hated Marshall. They'd banned him so

many times from their house and told him he wasn't worthy of her. Now he was desperate to prove himself to them. He was no longer a struggling no-hoper who'd got their daughter pregnant. He had fame and money beyond his wildest dreams.

'I'm going to marry Kim,' he said. 'She loves me. We have a child together. Be happy, please, Mom. I want your blessing.'

My problem is, I've never been able to say no to Marshall when he looks at me from under those long dark eyelashes. He's played me since the moment he was born. He knows I'll do anything to make him happy.

I told Marshall I had nothing to wear even though I knew it wasn't much of an excuse. He yanked open my closet doors, pulling out my clothes.

'How about this?' he asked, dragging out the long, blue, sleeveless gown I'd worn for my wedding to John Briggs the year before. I shook my head. I was in the midst of divorcing Briggs and I had no intention of ever wearing that dress again.

Marshall zeroed in on a gold-sequined gown I'd bought cheap from a tuxedo rental place that was going out of business. He held it up and said he loved it. Again I protested. The dress was completely inappropriate for a wedding. But Marshall said it was perfect.

The next few days zipped by in a flurry of activity. Sharon Spiegel, the minister at South Park Church who'd officiated at my marriage to Briggs as well as Tanya's wedding, agreed to conduct a small, simple ceremony. I was to stand up for Marshall, Bill would stand up for Kim. Nathan and Hailie were to be the only other guests.

The 15th of June dawned bright and sunny. Marshall drove Kim to the church. I followed with Nathan and Hailie ten minutes later. When I walked into the small brick building, it was packed. Mom was there with Dutch. There was Tanya and her new husband Lynard, her son Jonathan, his wife, their two children, my half-sister Betti Renee, her husband Jack, their three kids, my aunts Terri and Martha. Kim had invited them all. But at least her mother Kathy, her stepdad Casey and her twin sister Dawn weren't there.

I can barely remember the ceremony, I was so upset. There were no hymns and I don't recall a sermon. I focused on the minister Sharon's clothes. She wore a long dark skirt, shirt and sweater.

Kim had on a black micro-mini and a short cropped top. According to those sitting in the church, she didn't appear to be wearing any underwear.

After Marshall said 'I do', he picked up Hailie and held her in his arms for the rest of the service. Needless to say, Kim did not promise to obey Marshall.

The tears that had started trickling down my cheeks at the start of the ceremony were now cascading in waves. I could not stop crying. My legs felt like jelly: I could barely stand. I looked at Marshall and I just knew I had lost my son.

There wasn't a reception as such. Instead we just

headed to the drinking establishment where Tanya and Lynard had had their after-wedding do. Everyone but me was drinking. The bar owner closed the bar to the public so the newlyweds could have the place exclusively. He was also playing most of my son's music. I danced with Marshall, then I took Hailie home. I couldn't stand it any longer.

After the wedding, Marshall bought his first home. He was quoted in the press as saying the nearby trailer park reminded him of his roots. Later he told me he'd been misquoted; he had no idea there were mobile homes behind his mansion.

He also promised me they'd left my house in Casco Township clean and – after one earlier misunderstanding when he'd missed a payment because he was touring – there were no outstanding bills. But I got my brother Todd to pop over to check after they'd moved out. There were eviction notices stuck to the door and a pile of unpaid bills scattered around inside. The surrounding grass was tall and Todd had to cut it too.

Three police officers, called to the house by neighbours thinking Todd was an intruder, wanted to know if Eminem, the famous rapper, lived there. Todd tried to protect him, saying he thought some of Marshall's friends had been staying there while he was on the road.

I called Kim and asked what was going on.

'We don't want your damn trailer!' she snapped.

Her words cut me to the quick. It wasn't a trailer: it

was a big mobile home with a master bedroom and an *en suite* bathroom, and two other bedrooms. Now Kim had dumped out all my belongings, along with Marshall's drawings and demo tapes. She'd even thrown away home videos of her and Marshall. I told Todd to grab everything he could for safekeeping.

I jumped in my car for the 900-mile journey back to Michigan. The eviction notices and unpaid bills were all in my name. I needed a lawyer to sort everything out, to stop the repossession.

Fred Gibson had a big advert in the Yellow Pages, so I called, introduced myself, and said I needed help. He invited me to his office in Sterling Heights, telling me to bring over all the eviction documents. He was calm, assuring me he'd stop the foreclosure.

I turned up at Gibson's office a few hours later. It was a tall building, four or five storeys high, and I was impressed because he appeared to have an entire floor. Gibson was well over six foot, with dark-brown hair and a small moustache. He was well groomed, wearing an immaculate dress shirt and tie. He peered at me over his spectacles as I told him about the eviction notices and the trouble Kim caused. He asked me about Marshall and I told him all about the horrible *Rolling Stone* story. Gibson had not heard of Eminem at first, as he was just breaking out at the time.

Gibson was so sympathetic. He's baby-faced, boyish-looking. He seemed so nice, telling me he'd sort out the foreclosure and clear my name with the credit agencies.

Then he asked me to drop off the magazine articles so he could research and get up to date on everything.

Afterwards I drove to the house to meet an auctioneer. He was picking through the place, clutching tapes, a hairbrush and several toothbrushes. He wanted to know if they were Marshall's. He didn't say Marshall, of course. It was Eminem he was interested in. He seemed to think the stuff was valuable and could be sold at auction. Later, Kim tried to hold up the auction. Eventually it was held mid-week when hardly anyone was around. Kim demanded that I split the proceeds from the sale of the house with her. I tried to tell her I had to pay off the bank first, and that there probably wouldn't be much left over. She immediately called Marshall to tell him I was selling the place and planned to ask him if he would sign his name on the wall for the new buyer. Once again she was starting trouble for me.

For the first time it hit me: Marshall really was famous.

A few days later I drove back to Gibson's office with the magazines. I was keen to return to St Joseph, so he had me sign some papers. I filled in the usual details – my name, address, date of birth, social-security number. Then I scrawled my signature, shook his hand and left.

Every so often Gibson faxed me to say things were going well. When I phoned, he'd reassure me, saying, 'I'm the lawyer, let me do my job.'

On 17 September, Marshall called me screaming abuse.

He shouted, 'You're trying to take the food out of my daughter's mouth!'

I asked him to calm down. He was angrier than I'd ever heard him before. What, he demanded to know, was I thinking? Why was I suing him for $10 million? I had no idea what he was talking about. Then Nathan started yelling at me to turn up the television. I was all over the news: I was suing Marshall for defamation and emotional distress. I was in shock – and I felt like my life was spinning out of control.

# CHAPTER NINETEEN

I did not mean to sue my son for defamation; I just wanted to stop my home being repossessed and clear up the financial problems that had been caused. Gibson told me not to worry. He said that to sue Marshall for defamation would be a wake-up call to him, to stop him demeaning me in public. I felt as if I were in a bad dream and needed to wake up.

The last thing I wanted to do was upset my son. I didn't want his money. I had no idea where the figure $10 million came from either. According to the court papers Gibson filed at Macomb County Circuit Court, Michigan, I had suffered damage to my reputation, emotional distress, loss of self-esteem, humiliation and anxiety over statements Marshall had made in *Rolling Stone*, *The Source* and *Rap Pages* and on *The Howard*

*Stern Radio Show*. There was just a passing reference to my home being repossessed. But this was all true – my son was destroying me.

He stapled a retraction letter to the lawsuit, instead of mailing it to Marshall. Marshall's manager Paul Rosenberg fired back, saying, 'Eminem's life is reflected in his music. Everything he said can be verified as true. Truth is an absolute defence to a claim of defamation.

'His mother has been threatening to sue him since the success of his single "My Name Is". It is merely the result of a lifelong strained relationship between him and his mother. Regardless, it is still painful to be sued by your mother.'

Rosenberg and I never saw eye to eye on anything. Only I knew I had my son's best interests at heart, and I had not threatened to sue him over 'My Name Is'. I was terribly upset over the lyrics, especially the line where he makes comments about my breasts. That was horrible and upsetting because I'd contracted toxaemia – blood poisoning – when I gave birth to him and hadn't been able to breastfeed.

I thought the song was just plain silly. I actually thought he could have written something a lot better. Marshall said it was all a big joke, that no one believed the stuff he said was true.

Marshall and I were told that we were not allowed to respond in public over the lawsuit – everything had to be dealt with by our lawyers. But a record company executive telephoned me on one occasion.

'Do me a favour,' he said. 'Keep everything going. We're selling records.'

On another occasion Marshall rang, asking for the opposite.

'All I want for my birthday, for Father's Day, for Christmas and all the other holidays, is for you to drop the lawsuit,' Marshall said. 'I'll give you $25,000. I will look after you for the rest of your life.'

I did everything I could to stop the legal action. My life with Marshall, everything, was spinning out of control. My mother got in on the act. When Marshall asked her if he could use a snippet of his Uncle Ronnie rapping on a tape they'd made as teenagers, she threatened to sue him too. That I thought was odd. She'd spent the last year bragging to anyone who would listen that Eminem was her grandson and she'd brought him up alongside Ronnie. She'd even started selling Eminem T-shirts, claiming she had his blessing. Yet Mom was back and forth, first on my side and then against me. The whole family tried to get in on the picture.

Marshall hit back at my Mom, telling the *Detroit News*, 'My grandmother is going off on me. I loved Ronnie. I've got a Ronnie tattoo on my arm. I wanted to pay tribute to him.

'I let the public decide for themselves what idiots my family is. My family has never been there for me. They expect things because we're blood.'

Just about anyone who'd ever married into my family, be that a step-sibling, half-cousin or distant relative we didn't know existed, now wanted a piece of Marshall.

Bruce came out of the woodwork. He gave interviews saying he'd tried to stay in touch when our marriage broke up but had no idea how to find us. Considering that Bruce's own Aunt Edna and Nan – who had lived in the same house for fifty years – had always been a big part of Marshall's life, he hadn't looked very far. I wanted to scream that Marshall had written him letters, that he'd returned them unopened with the words 'Not known at this address' written across them. But, because of the stupid lawsuit, I couldn't say a word.

I'm told Bruce, along with his children Michael and Sarah, tried to go backstage to meet Marshall. He refused to see them, venting his fury on his next album, *The Marshall Mathers LP*, released in May 2000.

Claiming relatives were suing him or fighting over him, he makes reference to his half-brother and sister, who'd never tried to contact him until they saw him on television. But he reserved his worst words for me. Now I was an effing bitch mother who was suing him for every one of the pills he said he'd stolen from me. He claimed he'd picked up his habit from me, finding my medication under my mattress.

If ever I had to take prescribed medication, I sure didn't hide the fact, nor ever take anything illegal. With all that I'd been through in my life, of course I ended up in doctors' offices a few times, and was prescribed something for my nerves. I would've cracked if I hadn't have had something.

I was approached to put out my own CD with a hip-

164

hop group called Identity Unknown, or ID-X for short. If I couldn't defend myself in public over the lawsuit, I could do so via music. We met at a studio in Georgia and I was literally given five minutes to write an open letter to Marshall. It was originally called 'Set the Record Straight' but by the time it had been remixed three times it was called 'Dear Marshall'.

I started the poem by saying I still loved him but we had a problem, something had gone wrong between us.

'I was so excited by your success yet so let down by your betrayal,' I wrote, explaining how I'd tried to be mom and dad to him, giving him everything he ever wanted because he was perfect in my eyes.

'My unconditional love created a spoiled young man, an angry one too,' I wrote. I finished it with a plea that he'd stop his attacks, rewriting his lyrics, 'Will the real Marshall Mathers please stand up? And take responsibility 4 his actions.'

We flew to Nashville, Tennessee, and then drove to Georgia to complete the final remix. The CD was released to silence from the music press. It was available only on the Internet and to this day I have no idea how many copies it sold.

Nathan played it to Marshall. He thought one of the lines said, 'Poke your eyes out.' Nathan replayed it to him a couple of times to point out the proper lyrics.

*The Marshall Mathers LP* sold 1.7 million copies in its first week, knocking Britney Spears's *Oops!... I Did it Again* off the top of the charts. The first single, 'The Real

Slim Shady', had upset, among others, Christina Aguilera. She'd annoyed Marshall by letting slip on MTV that he was married. He responded by mocking her in his lyrics, claiming she had given him a sexually transmitted disease and had given oral sex to Fred Durst of Limp Bizkit and MTV's Carson Daly.

I felt sorry for Christina. She was only nineteen and had been vilified just like me. But, when asked on MTV if she was going to sue, she said, 'Suing for slander requires that somebody takes him seriously. It's obvious in the song that he's making this stuff up about a lot of people.'

The album also mocked *Baywatch* babe Pamela Anderson, her husband Tommy Lee, actor Will Smith, Britney Spears, N'Sync, the New Kids on the Block, Vanilla Ice and even Dr Dre. I was physically sick when I heard his reference to raping me on 'Kill You'.

His follow-up to his *The Slim Shady LP*'s '97 Bonnie and Clyde' – where he'd sampled Hailie's voice – was 'Kim'. He described it as a love song, describing his feelings when he discovered she was cheating. It ends with his choking her.

Needless to say, Marshall and Kim were having problems again. On 3 June he'd tailed Kim to a car-stereo shop, where he got into an argument with Douglas Dail, a road manager for his rap rivals Insane Clown Posse. Unbeknown to me, Marshall had started to carry a gun for protection. Dail claimed he waved it at him.

In the early hours of the next morning, Marshall

caught Kim kissing former bodyguard John Guerra in the parking lot of Warren's Hot Rocks Café. Again, Marshall brandished his gun. It wasn't loaded but, in the confrontation that followed, Guerra claimed Marshall hit him at least twice with the pistol and threatened to kill him. The police took both Marshall and Kim into custody. Marshall claimed he never pulled the gun on him; it fell out of his jogging pants.

Marshall told me later that the police officers asked for his autograph while they were fingerprinting him.

Kim was accused of breaching the peace. Marshall was bailed the following morning on assault and weapons-possession charges. But as he left the police station another officer called his cell phone. Dail had pressed charges over the previous day's incident.

I asked Marshall why he was carrying a gun. He claimed he needed it because he was always getting hassled.

'Son, where are your bodyguards?' I wanted to know.

It turned out his trusted security officer Byron Williams had been keeping a journal and planned to write a book about Marshall. My son was devastated. He thought Williams was a friend. He was so hurt, he'd dispensed with his bodyguards.

I couldn't believe he was roaming Detroit without protection and I was horrified that he was carrying a gun, regardless of whether or not it was loaded. He knew I hated firearms of any kind. My sister Tanya's husband Lynard had taught Marshall how to shoot a couple of years earlier. He'd become infatuated with guns.

Marshall was also worried about security at his house in Sterling Heights, across from the trailer park. It was on the main road, with just one small fence at the back that everyone climbed over. He often found fans in his swimming pool. Someone had set fire to his mailbox. He worried about going outside even to collect his newspaper.

The house had a long driveway but there was only one entrance. Fans blocked it with cars. When I dropped off Nathan, they tried to persuade me to take them inside. There were so many of them outside, it scared me.

Marshall covered his face when he went out, hoping he wouldn't be recognised.

A week after his arrest, Marshall was on stage in Portland, Oregon, when he announced that reports of his marriage problems weren't true, that Kim was in the wings. Then he pulled out an inflatable sex doll, committed a lurid act with it, threw it into the audience and encouraged everyone to beat up the 'Kim' doll.

On 7 July, while Hailie was watching TV downstairs with her cousin Lainie, Nathan, and Kim's mother Kathy, Kim smashed up her wedding picture and ornaments and tried to slash her wrists in the bathroom. She cut the wrong way and her wrists ended up in bandages.

Kathy called the police. Kim apparently told them, 'There has got to be a better place than this.'

All of this was colourfully covered by the world's media. Kim never gave interviews but she had written a letter to the *Detroit Free Press* after their June arrests saying, 'I don't think anybody in their right mind would cheat on a millionaire husband – especially with a nobody at a neighborhood bar.'

Now, no one who knows Kim took her suicide attempt seriously. She'd been creating dramas for years. She was forever locking herself in the bathroom, smashing mirrors and breaking everything else in her wake. Everyone usually ignored her.

Marshall decided it was time to send her a wake-up call. In August, two months after their first wedding anniversary, he filed for divorce, hoping it would shock her into calming down. That worked for a matter of days. She agreed to reconcile. Then *she* filed for divorce – and made it clear she was serious. Marshall was devastated.

Marshall says his life started to unravel in 2000. He'd been betrayed by his bodyguard, faced five or more years in jail, I was suing him, along with John Guerra, he was battling Kim for custody of Hailie, and he hated the fame he'd spent years seeking.

I agreed: 2000 was shaping up to be worse than 1999.

Nan, who was eighty-eight, had been in ailing health for some years. She weighed just 55 pounds (that's just 25 kilos, or 4 stone) and I knew we were losing her. She'd been the one constant in my life, the only real mother to me. As Nan's health worsened she and I had a talk about going to heaven. I assured her that if anyone deserved to go there it was surely her. Nan had devoted her whole life to helping out us kids and anyone else who came to her. She looked after me, Steve, Todd – all of us. I told her we didn't have to worry about that as she was going to be here for a long time yet. Sadly, I was wrong. Nan lived only three short months after that. I only wish I could have been there when she passed away. I was in Missouri when I got the call. It was one of the saddest days of my life.

Her death hit me so hard. She'd been born on 6 June 1912 – she hated all those sixes; even the year she was born divided into sixes – and had lived a long, hearty life. But it didn't make it any easier, losing her. She had lots more life to live – her last ten years had been very hard.

She'd been such a character. As a native American, she'd believed in natural medicine. I was stunned when she showed me a beautiful plant in her backyard. She said it was pot. Then she chopped it down and hung it up to dry. I worried she'd be arrested but she just laughed, saying, 'The police aren't going to go after an old woman like me.'

Nan, who'd grown up chewing tobacco, said she loved the smell of pot. She smoked it occasionally.

When she died her daughter Joyce took her ashes back to her native Alabama. She wanted me to ask Marshall to contribute towards building a memorial for Nan. Nan had always said she wanted to be buried at the foot of her brother in Michigan.

I was furious. Her wishes had been betrayed and now everyone expected Marshall to pay for everything. Nan would not have approved, either. She never took from anyone: she spent her life looking after others and she was always good at giving sage advice. I did wonder what she'd think of her foul-mouthed great-grandson and his fans, who'd taken to calling me a pig and spitting at me.

I'd got used to being recognised. With my mane of platinum-blonde hair I wasn't hard to spot. But until recently the fans had been polite, merely asking for autographs and snippets of gossip about my son.

Missouri is known as the American Bible Belt. Most people attend church yet the abuse I suffered was shockingly unchristian. One day at the East Mills shopping mall in St Joe two kids ran up to me, pulled the back of my hair, then spat at me. Nathan and I went to a movie theatre. The kids behind put chewing gum on the back of my seat and hair. Wherever I went, I was accosted by teenagers yelling abuse.

I stopped watching TV programmes about my son.

It was too upsetting. I was officially the most hated mother in America.

# CHAPTER TWENTY

Kim and Marshall briefly reconciled before once again formally separating. As if to copy me, she announced she was going to sue him for $10 million, claiming she'd been defamed by the lyrics on 'Kim'. They had no prenup and Kim made it clear she was not only seeking custody of Hailie, she was also going to take Marshall to the cleaners.

'I'm leaving your son. He won't pick up after himself. I am not his mother,' Kim said in a rare phone call to me.

I explained I'd always tidied up after him. She butted in and started screaming over and over, 'I am not his mother!'

Then she said she was moving into an apartment with Hailie and no one would ever know where they were.

She was on a spend-spend-spend spree. She thought

nothing of dropping $6,000 in fancy department stores such as Dillard's and Marshall Fields. She bought only expensive clothes.

Marshall had more clothes than he knew what to do with. He was flooded with free gear from companies keen for him to wear their brands. He gave bags of them to the Salvation Army.

Music pundits estimated Marshall was worth more than $30 million. I doubted that. But apparently he thought nothing of dropping $100 tips on drinks.

Before his split with Kim, he'd lavished presents on her mother and stepfather. He bought them cars, furs, leather coats, jewellery – the lot. He was still trying to appease them.

The press reported we weren't talking but we were. Our conversations were sometimes strained – I was still trying to drop my legal action again him – but, as always, he ended our calls by telling me he loved me. One Mother's Day, flowers arrived signed, 'Love, Marsh, your number one son'. He didn't spend money on me but I didn't care. The little things counted. Among my most treasured possessions was one of his posters that he'd signed for me just before he married Kim. He'd written on it, 'I love you even though you do more dope than I do. Ha, ha.'

He wasn't laughing over his split from Kim. On the phone, his voice was flatter and flatter. He always sounded so miserable.

'I love her,' he told me.

'I think she's a habit,' I said. 'And bad habits are hard to break. If you have any sense, you should run, not walk, away from her.'

He could have any girl in the world but the only one he wanted didn't want him. It broke my heart to hear him sound so miserable. I tried to explain that there were many more women out there, who would love him. But all he thought about was Kim's rejection. He'd known her since he was 15, that was almost half of his entire life. He was used to having her around.

Then there was Hailie and also Lainie, Kim's niece, whom he'd formally adopted. He feared losing both of them. I offered to care for them both but my half-sister Betti Renee and her husband Jack had become his live-in housekeepers. They watched over the girls when Marshall wasn't around.

They certainly weren't *my* idea of caretakers. I was furious that Betti Renee was even in the house.

Marshall said it was Kim's doing. She and Betti Renee loved to party. It didn't matter that Kim and Marshall had split – she still had a hold over everything he did.

Nathan wanted to spend Christmas with Marshall. He was really worried about his big brother. Marshall had given interviews saying he'd tried to overdose on painkillers shortly after Hailie was born but had thrown up. If this happened, he never told me about it. However, Nathan was now extremely worried about Marshall.

I spoke to Marshall on the phone and he sounded very depressed. Kim had played him for what he felt was the last time, and all the world had seen it. I told him we would drive from Missouri to his home in Michigan to see him. I quickly packed the car with clothes and Nathan and I set off.

But Betti Renee was there when we arrived. When I dropped Nathan off she had security order me off the premises. So I checked into a nearby Motel Six. I had stayed there in the past and got to know most of the help – they were always very accommodating.

Nathan returned early that evening, saying he didn't feel welcome at the mansion because there were so many hangers-on around. I rented a DVD player and invited over some of his old school friends, and we spent the rest of the week holed up at the motel watching old movies.

Nathan wanted to go on tour with Marshall. I really wasn't sure, but Marshall got on the phone to me and said, 'I promise there will be no alcohol, no dope smoking. I won't let him do any of that.'

When Nathan came back he told me there were *Playboy* bunnies and pretty girls everywhere and weed smoking on the tour bus. He said things that made my hair curl. I've always encouraged my sons to talk to me about everything. No subject has ever been taboo.

Marshall also fretted about the way Kim handled his fame. She was envious of them, complaining she couldn't go anywhere without being hassled. She didn't bother to hide the fact that she was seeing other men. She still had a hold over Marshall. He wasn't allowed to date, even though they were separated, but she did what she wanted.

Marshall put the Sterling Heights house up for sale. I'd never even been inside, as Kim had called security on me if I did anything other than drop off presents for Hailie or collect Nathan when he visited. I never usually got out of the car.

I went up to the house once and I could see it had marble floors and chandeliers when I peeked through the glass of the front door. But that was it. Marshall soon found another place on the Manchester Estates in nearby Clinton Township. It was a mansion inside a gated community, which meant he could keep the fans at bay.

Marshall's trial for pistol-whipping John Guerra was slated to start on Valentine's Day. He phoned me from Europe, where he was on tour, worried he was going to jail and wouldn't see Hailie for the next five years.

'Are you coming to the trial?' he asked.

Even though we were still involved in the lawsuit, and, according to the media that now accompanied Marshall wherever he went, we'd fallen out big time, I didn't hesitate. My son needed me. I'd have jumped in front of a train if he'd asked me to.

Nathan, who was now almost fifteen, was back on tour with Marshall. I still worried, even though he called to let me know he was OK most nights.

I feared for Marshall, too. At the start of his tour in Germany he'd gone on stage with a chainsaw, simulated murder and had apparently swallowed a handful of ecstasy pills. The next stop was Britain, where the police warned he'd be arrested if found with illegal substances.

It wasn't hard to keep up with news of my son. I had only to switch on the TV or pick up a newspaper to find out what he was doing. My phone at the taxi company was also ringing off the hook. Journalists from all over Europe wanted to interview me. Several simply turned up on at my door.

Britain's *Mail on Sunday* offered me the chance to set the record straight. Here's part of the article I wrote:

> I want to try to explain to his fans – and all the parents who I know are horrified by the lyrics in his songs – what makes my son tick. I want people to understand that the hate-filled rapper on stage is Eminem and not my boy Marshall.
>
> Basically, no one should take anything he says seriously – he doesn't mean it. He doesn't hate women or homosexuals and he's not violent.
>
> He is making money out of negative issues because he could not make it as a rap star any other way. When he first started to write filthy lyrics I asked him why. His answer was the more foul he was the more people loved him.

The European press had a field day with Marshall. They called him Public Eminem Number One. They likened his concerts to Hitler Youth rallies because he whipped up so much hatred with his homophobic and misogynistic songs.

Here's a piece that appeared in the *Daily Mail* just before he arrived in the United Kingdom:

> The Eminem phenomenon has divided the world. His violent lyrics, dripping with grotesque imagery and obsessive profanities, have appalled parents.
>
> Little wonder, perhaps, that American President George W. Bush once described him as 'the most dangerous threat to American children since polio'.
>
> Christian groups have despaired over his songs and their impact on young people. One influential American Rightwing preacher suggested that parents might need to arrange exorcisms for their children if they spent too much time listening to Eminem's music.

The article went on to say that kids didn't take his stuff seriously, that the crazed fan character on his latest hit 'Stan' was considered by some as a 'stunning commentary on modern celebrity'. Along the route, my son had also been compared to the poet Gerard Manley Hopkins and Elvis Presley.

Scotland's *Daily Record* traced his roots back to Edinburgh and suggested he could be descended from their national poet Robert Burns. They even quoted an expert saying they looked similar and were both famous for drunken bad behaviour!

The British *Daily Mirror* interviewed Bruce. Once again, he claimed I'd disappeared with Marshall and he'd spent years trying to find us. Part of the article read:

> Speaking from his modest flat near San Diego, California, the factory worker revealed he just wanted his angry rapper son to know he was after his forgiveness – not his money. His only memory of his son is a faded baby picture he took with him when he left.
>
> Struggling to control his emotions Marshall said: 'I desperately want to meet my son and tell him I love him. I'm not interested in his money. I just want to talk to him. I want him to know that I'm here for him if he lets me back into his life.'

He claimed to have just one grainy photo of himself holding his son as a toddler. That was something I found very odd because Marshall's baby book – which I'd left behind when we fled from Bruce – had somehow made its way to Germany. A magazine there had reprinted lots of pictures from it and quoted Bruce at length. Still, at least in the *Mirror* article, he acknowledged his past addictions, saying he now attended Alcoholics Anonymous and counselling sessions at a drink and drugs rehab centre.

180

Nathan returned from Europe, all excited about the places he'd been. He said Kim still managed to create havoc from 3,500 miles away, sparking a big bust-up when she could not get through on the phone to Marshall's hotel in Manchester. It also transpired that the British police had swooped on Marshall's so-called ecstasy pills. It turned out they were bits of dried-up chewing gum! Needless to say, I was relieved.

Marshall pleaded guilty to carrying a concealed weapon. I was furious. It meant he would have a criminal record. But he said his lawyers had struck a deal with the prosecutors, who'd agreed to drop the more serious charge of assault with a deadly weapon, which carried a four-year jail sentence. Even so, he still feared he'd be imprisoned and again asked me to be there for him at the next hearing.

At the beginning of April Nathan and I drove to Michigan and checked into a luxurious hotel near the Macomb County Court House. We hid away on the second floor; Marshall was on the ground floor. The staff were lovely, but early on they called me and asked if I could possibly pick up his clothes. There was stuff all over the floor and, because he was famous, they'd been told they could not move anything if they were to enter his room.

Marshall believed he'd be sent to jail because of who he was. But he insisted to me that he hadn't pistol-whipped Guerra.

'I hit him with my fist, the gun just fell out of my pants,' he told me. 'I swear, if I'd have hit him with the gun I'd have spit his head open. I was so angry.'

Nathan and I slipped into the back of the court just before the end of the hearing. The public benches were packed with kids wearing Eminem T-shirts. My heart was in my mouth as the prosecutor asked the judge to sentence Marshall to six months in jail. Marshall, looking the height of respectability in spectacles, a smart dark suit and tie, hung his head and showed no emotion.

The judge, Antonio Viviano, sided with the defence. He gave Marshall two years' probation, saying he had no previous criminal record and the gun wasn't loaded. He also ordered Marshall to pay $7,500 in fines and costs, banned him from possessing firearms and ordered him to submit to regular drug testing. Marshall was also barred from drinking excessively and had to get permission to leave the country.

'I consider probation to be punishment,' the judge warned him. 'I don't consider it a slap on the wrist. If you come back to this court, I can sentence you to up to five years in prison.'

Outside we all heaved a big sigh of relief. I hated the fact that Marshall had a criminal record but at least he wasn't jailed.

He still had to stand trial in nearby Oakland County on two weapons charges stemming from his run-in with Insane Clown Posse's Douglas Dail, and he was battling

*Above left*: Me with my brother Todd, 33, and Nathan, eight.

*Above right*: A studio photo of Nathan with a toy rabbit, taken while he was in foster care. This was given to me by my tearful son after one of his rare visits.

*Below*: Nathan stands beside my car after being released from foster care – I'd put a 'welcome home' placard on the side.

*Above*: Marshall in hand-painted 'M and M' outfit, on his stage debut with his band, aged 16 at Centerline High School.

*Below*: The 1979 classic Lincoln Town Car I gave Marshall for his 17th birthday.

*Above*: Marshall, aged 18, looking like Elvis Presley with Nathan on his fifth birthday in February 1991.

*Below*: Marshall, 18, with 14-year-old Kim. He's written 'Me and My Girl' on the back of the photo.

Marshall's very proud of his daughter.

*Inset*: Marshall's newborn daughter Hailie Jade Scott, early in 1996.

*Above*: Marshall – looking a bit chubby – with Nan in May 1998.

*Below*: Nan's house in Warren, Michigan. After it was sold, the new owner tried to sell it for $1 million because Marshall had spent some of his childhood there.

*Above*: Marshall blowing kisses at me on his tour bus in Lawrence, Kansas.

*Below left*: Me and Marshall on the tour bus at Lawrence.

*Below right*: Me, Marshall and Nathan at the gig.

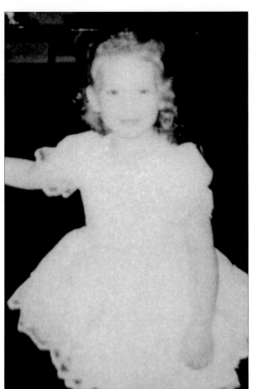

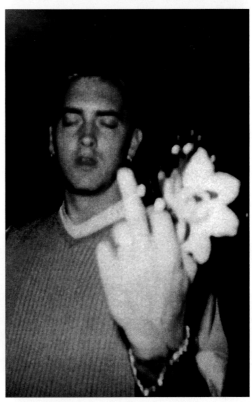

*Above left*: Hailie in a flower girl outfit at great aunt Tanya's wedding in June 1999. Her refusal to walk down the aisle prompted Marshall to propose to Kim so she could do her flower girl duties!

*Above right*: Kim and Marshall's first wedding with our friend Bill Hill.

*Below left*: Marshall kisses his bride. Meanwhile, I can't stop weeping.

*Below right*: The smiling groom gives the photographer the finger!

*Above left*: Me with Nan, three months before she died, January 2000.

*Above right*: Nathan posing in Marshall's rapper gear.

*Below*: My last Christmas together with Todd. *Inset:* The card for my brother's funeral service. I miss him terribly.

Kim, who'd filed for divorce in March, over custody of Hailie and money.

And first we had to sort out my lawsuit against Marshall. Every time I asked my lawyer to stop my lawsuit he said, 'It's come this far. We can't stop it now.'

Marshall offered me $25,000. He promised to send it direct to my lawyer, saying, 'I swear to God I will help you for the rest of your life. I just want you to stop this case.' I had already left a message, after my letters, and my calls were going nowhere.

Of course, I agreed. He knew I would do anything in the world for him.

I called Marshall's lawyer, Peter Peacock, and left a long message on his voicemail, saying I wanted to settle.

Then I turned to an attorney called Michael Marsalese. He agreed to help but we had only a matter of days before the case was due to be heard in Michigan. I waited back home in Missouri because I could not take time off from work. Michael called me and asked if I'd left a message for Marshall's lawyer. I said yes. Michael read my words back to me. He sounded furious. The court had a transcript.

I'd said, 'I'm going to be acting, I guess, on my own behalf. I understand that the offer would still be available to me for $25,000, and I will settle with Mr Gibson myself... I'd just like to see the case ceased, over and done with and put it to rest once and for all.'

Michael said he'd try to sort it out. I hadn't signed any agreement, it was all oral. I didn't care. I wanted it all to go away.

The judge ruled the $25,000 settlement was valid; the money was sent to the lawyers. All but $1,600 of it went in legal fees.

Marshall phoned me. 'I'm not sorry,' he shouted. 'Now you'll regret it.'

'Son, keep your money,' I said.

'No, I want you to have the money,' he yelled. 'You want to see how bad I can get. There's not a damn thing you can do about it.'

The line went dead. I could not get back through.

He changed all of his telephone numbers. I frantically tried reaching him through his management company, the studio, his staff, anything. He would not return my calls.

I'd lost Marshall out of my life over a silly misunderstanding.

# CHAPTER TWENTY-ONE

A few weeks later, I received a tape of Marshall's deposition. I could barely watch it. I was just so upset by everything. Marshall's people had told me to keep the court case going to sell records, but God only knows what they said to him about me. Now we were truly estranged and I cried all the time. The slightest little thing reduced me to tears. Marshall still phoned for Nathan but he refused to talk to me.

If I answered, he just snarled, 'Put me onto my brother.'

On other occasions he got his management to call. If I managed to intercept, he just said, 'Let me talk to Nate.'

I wasn't allowed to see Hailie. Marshall had threatened I'd never see her again. Now he stuck to his guns. I dropped presents – usually Barbie dolls that I knew she loved – at his house. I was told she didn't play with dolls any more. She was five and mixing pretend Martinis in her toy kitchen.

Marshall was back in court for sentencing in the Douglas Dail incident. He pleaded no contest to carrying a concealed weapon and brandishing a firearm in public. The judge, Denise Langford Morris, made headlines by rapping at him, 'Don't misstep, don't fall down. Now it's time for you to please stand up.'

She ordered him to do community service, pay $2,360 and sentenced him to a year's probation. Again, he had to submit to drug and alcohol tests but the judge added another rider: he had to get her permission to leave Michigan. Now it meant he couldn't even leave the state.

Nathan wanted to move back to Michigan because of Marshall. We needed a fresh start.

Marshall was playing at the Detroit Silver Dome. Nathan had several tickets and he wanted to go too. Despite everything, I was proud of my son and I just wanted to see him again.

But when we got to the box office there were no tickets. It turned out we'd mixed the dates up – we were due the following night. I managed to buy tickets from a scalper – or ticket tout – in the street. Once inside, I slid into my seat and hoped no one recognised me.

The show had barely begun when Marshall launched into an attack on me. He stood on the stage, shouted, 'Fuck you, Debbie!' and made an obscene gesture with his finger. A spotlight spun around the audience, then fell on me. The crowd erupted, some drunks behind us started jeering and swearing at me.

I was rescued by a reporter. She hauled me out and took me to the safety of the VIP area.

'You'll get hurt down there,' she said. 'A guy was pouring beer down your back.'

Needless to say, I did not attend the following night's concert. I was too upset. Later I found out that Marshall was disappointed. He thought I was going to be in the audience and had actually cleaned up his act.

'Why didn't she come? I didn't say, "Fuck you, Debbie!", so she'd have enjoyed it. I cleaned up my act for her,' he said, apparently unaware I'd been there the previous evening.

I reverted to using my maiden name – Nelson – for the first time since I was fifteen. I'd stuck with Mathers after my divorce from Bruce for Marshall's sake. Then I'd hyphenated it with Briggs when I married John. The world knew me as Debbie Mathers-Briggs. I hated it. I wanted everyone to get off my back. I figured no one would accuse me of being Eminem's mom if I called myself Nelson. Once again, I was wrong.

As I drove Nathan to school in November, we were hit head-on by a truck driver carrying over 5,000 lbs and speeding to beat the changing traffic lights. He said he didn't see us behind a van. The accident felt as if it was happening in slow motion, but there was nothing I could do to stop it. I braced myself for the impact, then I remembered nothing until I heard Nathan begging me to get up. I'd been knocked out by the air bag exploding. Everything was hazy, like smoke. The front of my car was all smashed up, Nathan's side had taken the brunt of it. He had blood all over his sleeve.

A policeman who had jumped in behind my seat was holding my head and ears really tightly. He thought I'd broken my neck. But I tried to get up to reach Nathan because of all the blood on him.

'No, Mom, it's not me bleeding. It's you,' he said. His legs were pinned under the dashboard and he remained trapped inside the car while I was stretchered into the ambulance.

I'd been at the hospital for four hours waiting to get stitches above my right eye when Mr Daniels, an old handyman we knew, arrived. Nathan had called him. He said the media were camped outside. We had to sneak out the back, with me lying down to avoid the press.

We were reunited with Nathan back home. He was distraught because the guy who hit our car had said to him, 'Sorry about your mom. Did she die?' as he was leaving the police station.

Again there'd been sniggering among the police officers in front of Nathan about how hated I was. It was so cruel. Nathan had got my brother Todd and Mr Daniels running all over trying to find me at various hospitals. No one would tell them anything because of who my son Marshall was.

When Kim filed the divorce papers in March she claimed the relationship had broken down so badly that 'there remains no reasonable likelihood that the marriage can be preserved'. She wanted full custody of Hailie, along with an extortionate $2,740 a week in child support, a new mansion and $10 million to settle her defamation suit against Marshall.

After seven months of legal wrangling, they finally settled. The judge sided with Marshall, ordering him to pay $1,000-a-week child support. They agreed to joint custody: he kept the Clinton Township mansion, which was valued at $450,000, and she was to receive $475,000 to buy her own place nearby. Marshall's earnings were put at $2.7 million a year and the terms of the defamation settlement were to remain secret. I'm pretty sure she got a hefty sum.

But at least Kim's case for sole custody of Hailie – the one weapon she always used against my son – had been seriously weakened by an arrest for possession of cocaine. She had two previous drink-driving convictions, so, when the police stopped her for a routine traffic check and discovered the drugs, even Kim knew she was in trouble. As always when she was arrested, she assumed Marshall would sort it out. Suddenly, he was a big important guy in Michigan.

Some years earlier she'd called from jail to say she'd been rounded up with a group of other women by vice squad detectives who'd raided the Oasis health spa. She claimed she was working there as a receptionist. As always with Kim, there was no way of telling what was true and what wasn't.

I hoped Marshall could now put the Kim shenanigans behind him. He was enjoying success beyond his wildest dreams – along with his old Detroit pals D-12, he'd topped the charts with their debut album *Devil's Night* and the single 'Purple Pills', and he was secretly dating the megastar singer Mariah Carey.

Now, I don't have any personal anecdotes about Mariah, since Marshall and I weren't talking. But I do know they originally planned to collaborate on a song, which would have been a hoot considering their different personalities. That never happened, but they saw each other on and off for a while.

That he'd fallen for Mariah didn't surprise me. She looks a lot like Kim. Marshall always goes for a certain type of woman: tall, blonde and big-boned. I think Mariah has a beautiful voice, so I was happy for them both.

Unfortunately, they got together just before her very public nervous breakdown in July. She'd just split from her long-time boyfriend Luis Miguel and Marshall was finally free from Kim. Apparently, she flew to Detroit in her private jet to persuade Marshall to appear in the video for her song 'Glitter'. He kept her waiting on the tarmac for four hours, before telling her he didn't want to work with her.

Despite the rejection, there was obviously a spark of romance between them. A few weeks later they got together at her New York apartment. They went out with a crowd that included the rappers Eve and Run DMC, drinking champagne until dawn at a Manhattan club, and the rumour mill buzzed with talk of an affair. Both had publicists deny they were anything but friends.

Then she cracked up. After leaving a series of rambling messages for fans on her own website, she was admitted to hospital suffering from extreme emotional and physical exhaustion. A romance with my son was probably the last thing she needed at that point but the relationship continued after she was released from the clinic.

Unfortunately, she didn't act bizarrely only on her website posting: she left rambling messages on Marshall's voicemail, too. He let it be known he'd kept them. It didn't take long for word to get back to Mariah that he'd been dissing her to his showbiz friends.

To this day, Mariah denies they ever did anything other than hang out together a few times. Marshall, being Marshall, gave an interview to *Rolling Stone* after they'd split, saying, 'I don't really like her as a person. She doesn't really have it all together.'

Mariah responded in the British *News of the World*'s *Sunday* magazine with, 'I spoke to him on a regular basis but it was not a relationship. I find it pretty surprising that he would actually misrepresent something like that.

'In general terms I think that men who have to lie about having a sexual relationship, who misrepresent a friendship, must have an underlying reason for doing that. It's curious to me.'

She made no secret of the fact that a track called 'Clown', on her comeback album *Charmbracelet*, was

191

aimed at Marshall. She claimed they'd never even touched each other and the lyrics included the lines, 'You don't want the world to know... the little boy inside often sits at home and cries.'

Mariah told *Sunday*, 'A lot of girls identify with that song, we've all met clowns.'

The feud escalated when Marshall played back one of her answer-machine tapes on his Anger Management Tour. In a whiney, pleading voice she'd begged him to contact her, saying, 'I heard you were getting back with your ex-wife? Why won't you see me? Why won't you call me?'

I felt sorry for Mariah but, when it came to Kim, no other woman stood a chance. She had a hold over my son because of Hailie. And there was more to it than that. Marshall doesn't like change. As we've seen, he's known Kim since he was fifteen; he's used to her madness and abuse. She's a habit he just can't seem to break.

# CHAPTER TWENTY-TWO

Kim Basinger played me in *8 Mile*, the fictionalised film of Marshall's life. In the movie, the straggly-haired, drunken, drug-addicted mother comes on to her son and tries to hit on his friends. No doubt the rumours of an off-screen relationship between Marshall and his co-star, who's eighteen years his senior, were good for publicity for the movie. But the actress who totally had the hots for my son during filming was Brittany Murphy.

She spent a lot of time hanging out at Marshall's mansion. I didn't get to meet her but I saw the way she looked adoringly at him at awards shows and film appearances. He was flattered but she isn't his type.

Brittany is a tiny little thing – much smaller in real life than she appears on screen. She reminded me of Amy, the girl Marshall was dating when Kim got pregnant. If I could have picked a wife for my son it would have been Amy. I adored her.

Now Byron Williams, the bodyguard who betrayed my son by writing a book called *Shady Bizzness*, claimed Marshall had an appetite for very young groupies. There are pictures in his book of Marshall surrounded by girls. I think it's all a big show, my son hamming it up for the cameras.

Williams also had some harsh words to say about Kim. In an interview with Britain's *Sunday Mirror*, he said, 'I saw her throw a lamp at Eminem on a tour bus, knocking him down. Man, he is terrified of her. She is one tough lady and bigger than him. I worry that either she is going to kill him or he is going to kill her.'

Williams also worried about Marshall's drug use, telling the newspaper, 'He was like a one-man walking pharmacy. I can recall one day where he took fourteen different drugs. It started with ecstasy for breakfast, then liquor, Vicodin, valium, magic mushrooms, marijuana, Tylenol 3 and a host of other over-the-counter drugs.'

As a mother, I find that a frightening thing to hear. The media said he'd sometimes taken thirteen ecstasy tablets a day and that he had no memories of 1999, the year he first made it big. According to them, the tours, hits and adulation were all a blur to him.

My friends often ask why I read anything that's written about my son. They know how upset I get. I breeze through the stuff because sometimes it's the only way I can find out what he's going through. Williams witnessed him crying with frustration. He said his fame, money and marriage had made him miserable. The only thing that made him happy was Hailie.

I still tried to reach out to Marshall. I wanted him to know I was there for him. It broke my heart that he was in so much pain. But my calls were met with silence.

Bizarrely, Bruce's ex-wife Lesley and his daughter Sarah – Marshall's half-sister – contacted me. They seemed to think I could fix a meeting. Sarah said she first noticed Eminem on MTV and thought he was the spitting image of her own brother Michael. She put it down to coincidence until *Rolling Stone* printed a picture of me holding Marshall as a baby. When she showed her father he apparently recalled his long-forgotten son. Both Lesley and Sarah knew he had a child from his first marriage. They said they remembered the letter that Bruce sent back unopened.

They were both nice people but in one conversation Sarah asked me, 'Do you think I can ask Marshall for a car?' adding she was only joking, she only wanted to meet him.

'Oh, honey, please don't,' I said, explaining that everyone wanted a piece of my son.

Marshall was once greeted backstage at a concert by a bunch of kids waving birth certificates, claiming to be related on his father's side. He brushed them off and I don't blame him.

Bruce and I had an odd phone conversation. He said he 'vaguely' remembered our marriage. I asked why he kept telling the press lies: that I'd disappeared and he could not find us. He changed the subject. I asked how many children he had. I'd heard that Heather, the last girl he cheated on me with in North Dakota, had had children by him. There were rumours of several others. For all I knew, Marshall had seven or eight half-siblings. Bruce said he had three or four kids – he didn't seem sure.

'You're a piece of work,' I said, then put the phone down.

It wasn't just family members who acted oddly around Marshall. He called a doctor because he had a high fever. The man arrived with his son and a camera. After taking pictures, they left.

'Hell, he forgot all about me,' Marshall said. 'Now I'm going to have to call him back to treat me.'

DeAngelo Bailey, who'd bullied Marshall at Dort Elementary, got in on the act. He announced he was suing Marshall for $1 million for invasion of privacy and slander. He claimed the 'Brain Damage' lyrics had harmed his aspiring rap career and made him an object of mockery.

Then Kim dropped a bombshell on him. She was pregnant. She refused to name the father but it transpired he was Eric Hartter, who'd done prison time on drug charges. Marshall was furious on Hailie's behalf. He didn't want a drug dealer anywhere near his daughter and threatened once again to apply for sole custody.

When he wasn't caring for Hailie, Marshall worked flat out. He buried himself in the studio, working on the soundtrack for *8 Mile*, his upcoming solo album and producing for others.

Nathan, who was almost sixteen, was also working on his career. Jimmy Mann, one of the attorneys who'd helped me during the Fred Gibson–Marshall case, became our manager. Jimmy helped field calls for me – there was a constant stream of calls from TV shows wanting me to appear.

Bruce Goodison was an acclaimed British documentary maker. He wanted to do a fly-on-the-wall film for the BBC called *Eminem's Mum*. He continually called Jimmy and Michael until I agreed that Nate and I would do it. I was truly pleased to see he put my brother Todd in it too. He followed us everywhere we went and allowed us all to be ourselves.

He flew into Detroit with Rosie his assistant and spent several months tailing me. We had a blast. Rosie and Nathan really hit it off. Bruce was a gentleman. He teased me because I always seemed to have a cigarette in my hand when the camera was on me.

Early on, Bruce said, 'After everything I'd heard about you I thought I was going to meet a horrible, evil beast. But you are the sweetest, most down-to-earth person.'

I was still recovering from the November car crash, in constant pain and worried how my damaged eye would look on screen. Nathan showed them photos of my battered face. My doctors told me that with the injuries to my head and back, I could not work. So now I became a TV star by default.

Their film culminated with Nathan's sixteenth birthday on 3 February. I rented a hall for $1,700, ordered lots of buffet food and invited all of our friends. Marshall agreed to come – he wouldn't miss Nathan's birthday for the world.

Dad and Geri were invited to Nate's birthday party. I was very upset as they only seemed to come in order to get photos with Marshall. I felt he was never accepted by them until he became famous, and they completely forget about Nathan. I spent most of the evening trying to stop everyone buying alcohol for Nathan, who was performing on stage. Then, just before Marshall arrived, he sent his people in to scope the place out. I'd told the BBC film crew they couldn't film, and it angered them but I was not about to jeopardise Nathan's sixteenth birthday party for the world. Everyone else was ordered not to take pictures or video too. There was no way I wanted Marshall upset – this would be his first appearance since I had attended his court case ten months before.

Marshall swanned in and immediately accused me of taking photos of him. Of course, I had a camera. It was Nathan's birthday. But I hadn't taken any of Marshall except the ones he approved of with my dad and him. He cursed me as he had everyone's attention by then. I wanted to die. I would never do anything to harm him with pictures.

'I told you to fucking stop taking pictures!' he shouted.

'I'm not taking photos,' I said.

'Give me the fucking camera!' he yelled.

Box, Marshall's bodyguard, tried to calm him down. But I ended up in tears as Marshall stormed off. It was so unfair. This was Nathan's big sixteenth birthday, and it was ruined. I retreated into the ladies' room to collect myself.

Marshall was under tremendous stress, although I didn't know why at the time. It turned out the release date for his new album, *The Eminem Show*, kept getting put back as he worked flat out on it, as well as the soundtrack for *8 Mile*.

The movie itself had wrapped; reaction in Detroit and Warren was mixed. The worst bit of Downtown Detroit is a ghost town of boarded-up buildings, weed-infested lots and barbed wire. The eerie silence is broken only by gunfire and police sirens. In 1996 the city earned the dubious title of 'the world's least appealing travel destination'. Not much had changed since then. The population continued to plummet as the crime rates rose. The suburbs sprawl as far as Flint, some sixty miles away, and, as in every city in America, there are good and bad areas.

Naturally Marshall's Michigan fans loved it that Hollywood's spotlight had fallen on Detroit. The movie production had helped the local economy. Some people hoped that might revitalise Downtown. Others fumed that *8 Mile* would do nothing to improve outsiders' views of the once majestic motor city.

Marshall responded to his critics in an interview with

*The Face*, saying, 'The fucking white-trash capital of the world. I'm white trash, so what the fuck? You can't tell me. I grew up in it.'

He'd made a few comments about me, too, saying most mothers would be happy to have Kim Basinger playing them but I was bitching about it.

'Anyone else would probably take that as a compliment. But I don't think my mother will,' he told *Blender* magazine.

He never asked my opinion. If he had, I'd have told him I thought I was delighted Kim was playing me. I think she's a wonderful actress, as well as being really pretty.

Marshall insisted the film was fiction. He was playing a make-believe character called Jimmy Smith. In fact, there's a disclaimer saying that at the end of the movie. Yet most people assume it's his life story.

Marshall had warned me I'd learn just how bad he could be in our final conversation after we'd settled the Fred Gibson case. He was as good as his word. 'Without Me', the first single from *The Eminem Show*, went straight for the jugular. He used his 'Fuck you, Debbie' line. It broke my heart when I heard it. He no longer called me Mom, I was fuckin' Debbie.

Lynn Cheney, the Vice President's wife, Limp Bizkit and Moby were also parodied. The song went straight into the *Billboard* charts at Number 2.

The accompanying video had Marshall playing Batman and Robin – just as he'd done as a child charging alone

200

around the house in interchanging capes. It co-starred Nathan, as young Marshall. Then Marshall himself donned a big blond wig and appeared to be mimicking me on a Jerry Springer-style TV show. By the time the scene switched to Marshall dressed as Osama bin Laden I couldn't see for the tears streaming from my eyes.

'Cleanin' Out My Closet (I'm Sorry Mama)' seemed – at first – to be Marshall's way of apologising to me. In the chorus he said he'd never meant to hurt me. Then in the second verse he turned on his father. So far, so good. But Marshall had saved the worst lines until last. He told of watching me taking pills, claimed he was a victim of Munchausen syndrome by proxy and was made to believe he was ill when he wasn't. He goaded me about making my own CD, said Nathan would soon realise I was a phoney and that I would not be allowed to see Hailie growing up.

He ended with the lines that he hoped I'd burn in hell because, when Ronnie had died, I'd said I wished it was him instead. Now, according to Marshall, he was dead to me.

In the heat of the moment – when I'd just buried Ronnie, and Kim had got rid of my furniture – I had said I wished Marshall was dead. But I'd apologised immediately and probably hundreds of times since. I'd been so upset over my little brother's death and Kim had wound me up. The words just tumbled out of my mouth. I thought Marshall had accepted I didn't mean it. But here he was, ten years later, throwing it back in my face, telling the world what I'd done.

# CHAPTER TWENTY-THREE

I bought *The Eminem Show* because I always try to support everything Marshall does, but I drew the line at attending screenings for *8 Mile*. I knew I could not sit through it. Even so, I was so proud of him in November 2002, when he became the first artist ever to top the movie, album and singles charts at the same time. He added another string to his bow at the 2003 Academy Awards when 'Lose Yourself' became the first rap song to win a music Oscar.

By the end of 2003 – just four short years into his career – Marshall had racked up seven Grammy awards, two MTV movie awards for *8 Mile*, nine MTV music awards and eight MTV Europe music awards. He'd also made *The Guinness Book of Records* as the fastest-selling rap artist ever. He'd sold 40 million albums worldwide and 'Lose Yourself' was his most successful single, spending twelve weeks at the top of the American chart.

When he was first nominated for a Grammy in 2000, he didn't even bother attending the ceremony, assuming he wouldn't win. He felt the same about the Oscars, declined an invitation to perform 'Lose Yourself', and later said he was fast asleep when the show went out on live TV.

*8 Mile* opened to great acclaim. The *Los Angeles Daily News* awarded it three and a half stars, saying,

> It's a great bet, and director Curtis Hanson (*LA Confidential*) is smart enough to use Eminem's ferocious wit and charisma to create a wildly entertaining movie that stands as the hip-hop generation's very own *Saturday Night Fever*. *8 Mile* isn't exactly autobiographical... So the movie both hews to the facts of Eminem's life – the rags-to-riches story, the contentious relationship with his mother (played here by Kim Basinger), the brutal, funny and outrageous one-on-one rap battles where he honed his craft – and aims to do repair work on his media image.

Of course, all the reviews mentioned Basinger's portrayal of the mother as a hard-drinking deadbeat with a lover young enough to be her son. It didn't matter that Universal were at pains to point out that the story was fiction – everyone assumed her part was based on me.

I knew I wouldn't be able to see the film in a public cinema, as I knew I'd get too upset, so I waited until it came out on DVD. I've tried to watch it but every time I put it on it makes me sick. I'd never seen it all the way through, just bits and pieces, until the summer of 2007. Everyone kept telling me I should watch it because it was fiction and not real life. I was still upset but I managed to watch to the end.

The Basinger character comes onto her own son and his friends. That is just sick. She's addicted to drink and bingo, her trailer is an absolute pigsty. Now, I don't drink. And I'm compulsive when it comes to keeping my house clean. People tease me for straightening out cushions the moment someone stands up, or emptying ashtrays the second someone puts out a cigarette. Kim's family lived just off 8 Mile, for most of their lives as I'm told. Marshall and I only once briefly had a home in Detroit just off 8 Mile when I bought our first house on Dresden, on the Detroit-Warren border.

*8 Mile* renewed interest in me. Once again newspaper and magazine articles appeared saying that I never worked, that I pretended things had happened to me in shops so I could sue. I have never sued Wal-Mart, the dollar stores or any other retail establishment for that matter. I have heard that other members of my large, extended family have done that, but definitely not me.

I did try to take legal action against Dort Elementary School after Marshall was bullied by DeAngelo Bailey. The staff had done nothing to protect him. And his

205

medical bills were enormous, so of course I wanted those paid. But the judge ruled schools were immune from lawsuits. I took it all the way to Lansing, the state capital, and I know my battle at least helped get things changed. I'd gathered petitions at school gates because most parents were unaware that schools would not guarantee children wouldn't be harmed. As we saw earlier, after my fight, schools took out insurance policies for parents to buy.

Marshall was recovering from that beating when he got food poisoning from a hotdog. He ended up in hospital on an IV drip. I took the remaining sausages to the hospital technicians for testing. Sure enough, they were bad. I called the store manager to get him to pull the brand from the shelves. He offered me a free case of hot dogs. I declined. Marshall and I did not want to ever see a hot dog again after he'd been so ill. Then we were offered $1,500, which of course I took. I needed it to cover the medical bills. But Marshall demanded the money should go to him. In the end I gave him $200 or $300 – I forget how much exactly – and the rest went towards our bills.

Now, aside from the Fred Gibson lawsuit against Marshall, there were only two other occasions when I sued someone. Again, it was just after Marshall had been hurt at Dort Elementary. I was doing some modelling to make money and my mane of long blonde hair was my image. I went to get a trim but the stylist, for some reason, took an instant dislike to me. She was heavy-set and demanded to know if I'd always been skinny. Then she hacked my hair off. Before I could stop her, I had a short back and sides and a Cleopatra fringe. Then she laughed in my face, saying she'd only done as I asked. There was a place that bought hair to make wigs for kids with cancer. I guess she planned on selling it there. I was so upset, I did take her to court. I did not want her doing it to anyone else. The judge awarded me $1,500.

Then I went to a dentist for root-canal surgery. I'd never had major work done on my mouth before, so I did not know what to expect. When I came round from the anaesthetic, a nurse was stitching up my gum. She told me to bite on a tea bag when I got home to stem the bleeding and gave me a prescription for sleeping medication. I was in agony – I couldn't stand up and I practically crawled out of the surgery. Back at home I couldn't understand why my mouth felt so odd, as if something was missing. The dentist had pulled four of my teeth on the upper right side.

I had to have expensive oral surgery to sort out that mess. The dentist was eventually done for twenty-seven counts of malpractice. My tooth extraction was the bottom of the pile but I eventually got $1,500. Again, it did not cover the medical bills I had to pay to correct the painful mistakes he'd made.

By the time *8 Mile* came out I was suffering a very different type of pain: empty-nest syndrome. Marshall never left home. He was twenty-six with his own child when I left him to marry John Briggs. Nathan was a different kettle of fish. His childhood was much harder than Marshall's. I'd brought him up single-handed. He'd never enjoyed the holidays in Florida, Canada or Tennessee that we'd had with his father Fred. Nathan never understood why Fred had been so good to Marshall but didn't want to know him. I couldn't explain it to him either. I too was hurt that Fred abandoned us. Then I lost Nathan for sixteen months to foster parents. And, when he was fourteen, his big brother had exploded onto the rap scene, making him grow up fast.

Nathan went on tour with Marshall, but it was hard for him to make genuine friends. He never knew whether someone liked him for real or just wanted to get close to Marshall. He was also working on his own rap act but worried constantly that people compared him unfavourably to his brother.

Marshall used to protect Nathan from bullies but once he was on probation he couldn't do that because he could not risk getting into trouble again. Nate befriended one young man who protected him for a while. But then he started to steal things from Nathan such as his shoes and a camcorder. When a Rolex that Marshall had given him went missing, Nate vowed to stick with the two pals he'd been close to since before Marshall was famous. He felt they were the only people he could really trust.

It didn't help that Marshall and I were no longer speaking. But Nathan acted as the go-between, keeping the lines of communication open.

I did everything I could to make Nathan happy. I

bought a house in Fraser, a small Macomb County community fifteen miles from downtown Detroit, and converted the basement into Nathan's quarters. Aside from his bedroom, there was a pool table down there, with a big-screen TV and his own phone so that he'd feel as if it were his own separate apartment.

He was crazy about a girl, a model who was two years older than he was. She was incredibly pretty, with exotic, dark, Italian colouring that matched Nathan's olive complexion. They made a cute couple and I was happy for her to hang out in Nathan's basement.

Then, on Nathan's seventeenth birthday, I had an odd feeling all day that something was wrong. Call it a mother's instinct. I was at the doctor's having a series of tests – I was still suffering head pain from the 2001 car crash – when I just had a gut feeling that something bad was happening at home. I can't explain how I knew, I just knew.

I abandoned my medical tests and rushed home. Nathan was nowhere to be found. I phoned everywhere, even Fraser Police. I thought he'd been kidnapped. With Marshall's fame, along with his enemies in the rap world, I never knew what to expect. The police couldn't do anything: at seventeen, Nathan was an adult.

Eventually, he was tracked down to the girl's parents' house. He'd decided to move in with them, after a lot of coaxing. This didn't last long; Nathan soon returned home, but those few weeks seemed like an eternity to me.

I'd read all about empty-nest syndrome, but no one

prepared me for the shock of it. From 1972, when I was seventeen, my life had revolved around children. For thirty years I'd cared for and nurtured first Marshall, then Nathan, along with the kids I'd fostered and all their pals. Then, suddenly, nothing. I hated being alone in the house. The silence was unbearable. I was so used to the sound of both my sons. There'd always been a stereo or radio playing somewhere. Their friends had become my friends. They would still phone often but that still wasn't enough.

I understood Nathan wanted to grow up, to stand on his own two feet, but it was so hard for me. I did everything I could to keep myself busy, to make up for the emptiness I felt inside. I took in Joey, an old friend who's partially sighted, and spent hours visiting other elderly people who needed help. I threw myself into renovating my home, did volunteer work for Amnesty International and Mothers Against Drunk Drivers.

Nathan dated a lot of very pretty girls. I guess he wanted to see if they cared about him for who he was, and not just because he had a famous brother. But I'm not sure why my sons seem to make such poor choices when it comes to women. When asked by *The Face* how many times he'd fallen in love, Marshall said, 'Once. And that's enough for me.'

I understand that Kim has a hold over him because of Hailie but he has never made much of an effort to find anyone else. I don't think he likes change. Kim has always loomed large in the background.

Six months after she gave birth to Eric Hartter's daughter Whitney in 2002, Kim returned to Marshall. He took them both in but it didn't take long for the trouble to start again.

In the early hours of 10 June 2003, Kim was stopped by police for driving erratically. The officers found two bags of cocaine in her car and one on her. Marshall, who was on tour, flew back to Detroit by private jet to ask a judge for full custody of Hailie.

Then, in September, police raided a party she was throwing at Warren's Candlewood Suites Hotel. She admitted her guests had taken ecstasy and marijuana and was charged with maintaining a drug house.

Warrants for her arrest were issued when she failed to show up in court on 7 November. Five days later Marshall was awarded temporary full custody of Hailie.

Kim finally turned herself in on 19 November. She faced a long jail sentence but to my surprise she was asked to post only $53,000 bail. However, she was ordered to wear an electronic tag and go to drink- and drug-counselling sessions. The following month she struck a plea bargain with prosecutors and was given two years' probation.

I received a verbal invitation from Nathan to Hailie's eighth birthday party on Christmas Day. I was so excited. The party was at a roller-skating rink. Nathan warned me that Marshall had laid down some ground rules: I wasn't to smother Hailie, I had to let her skate and play with her friends. I was more than happy to oblige and spent the next few days shopping for gifts. I bought her several Barbies, because she always loved them, and some baby dolls. But I felt as if people were sneering at the presents I'd given her. She had so many gifts, each one bigger and more elaborate, that she seemed overwhelmed.

But she was so pleased to see me that she kept breaking away from her friends to come over and talk to me.

Marshall kept staring at me. I hoped he'd break the ice by coming over to chat. When it became apparent he wasn't going to, I made my way to his table and asked how he was.

'Fine,' he replied.

That was it. He wouldn't even look me in the eye. He was like a mime puppet, straight-faced, motionless. I felt so awkward in front of him. He was my son, someone I loved so much it hurt. We'd always talked about everything. Now he sat in front of me with a frozen, hard expression. I walked away and found a bench to sit on when a lady came over to introduce herself. She was one of Marshall's neighbours on the Manchester Estates. She was curious as to why my son was behaving like a puppet even towards his managers. I couldn't answer that.

I knew I'd cry if anything else happened, so I went over to Hailie to say goodbye.

'I love you, Fuss Bucket,' I said, giving her a big cuddle. She giggled, but Marshall cut in.

'Don't call her that,' he snapped. 'She's not a baby.'

Then he handed me an envelope and told me not to open it until I was outside.

The moment I got to my car I tore it open. Inside was $500 and a Christmas card with a reindeer on the front that read, 'Debbie, love, your son Marshall, Nathan, Hailie, Alaina and Kim.'

That was it. I was no longer Mom: I was merely Debbie. I sat in the car, watching them all leave the rink with presents and balloons. Then I drove home, crying all the way.

# CHAPTER TWENTY-FOUR

I was driving back from a friend's on 22 January 2004 when I stopped at a gas station on the junction of 8 Mile and Coolidge Road to fill up my Honda Accord. It was just after 11 p.m., the cashier had dimmed the lights and I had to try several times before I could get my credit card to work. I paid in advance and started to fill the car up. I left the nozzle pumping into my tank, then sat back in the driver's seat to make a note of my mileage.

Suddenly there was a clunk that sounded like the nozzle falling, then a guy shoved his arm through my window. He put a gun in my face.

'Get the fuck out!' he growled.

I couldn't believe what was happening. It was all in slow motion, like a movie.

'But you're just a kid,' I said, stunned by his youth.

The kid had chipmunk cheeks; he was baby-faced. But his eyes were glassy.

'Bitch, I'm not playing,' he snarled.

I shook as I tried to grab my purse. Papers fell everywhere, all over the floor. Weird thoughts went through my mind: aside from the money – I had $3,573 on me in cash and an emergency $100 bill in a secret compartment of my wallet – I didn't want him to get every last stitch of my personal ID accumulated over my life. These included many old driver's licences, my boys' first paper licences, their birth bands, many pictures and letter, my identity papers and even articles I had gathered for my book. Most of it was in my large purse, so full I couldn't even close it.

My life flashed in front of me. I thought, My God, I didn't get to talk to my sons. Marshall will never believe this. What am I going to do if I get shot?

It was like being in the middle of a bad dream that seemed to go on for ever, although in reality it all happened in seconds.

My beloved dog Itchy, a Labrador mix, was also in the car. I grabbed his leash. The kid finally yanked me from the car, grabbing my hair and vigorously shaking my head back and forth before throwing me onto the ground beside the pumps. Itchy landed on top of me, and I nervously wrapped his leash around my coat. He pressed the gun – a small silver .45 pistol – to the dog. I screamed 'No, not the dog!' and, with his nerves showing, he put the gun back on me while mumbling something about

216

his daddy being in Jackson and he wanted to be there with him. Then he started repeating 'Goodbye, bitch.'

'Please, please, no!' I cried.

'Bitch, I don't play games,' he snarled. 'I'm going to kill you. Say goodbye.'

He clicked the gun. Nothing happened. He hit the bottom of the gun with his hand, swearing and cursing. He told me to get up and run backwards. I managed to get on my feet but immediately felt as if I was going to collapse. Once again he came back at me with the gun, telling me to say goodbye. But then he ran, jumping into my car. There was a squeal of tyres and the kid took off in my car with all of my things.

The cashier was hovering inside. I went running in but he ordered me to take the dog and get out. I begged him to call the police. He put the phone in the opening of the bullet-proof window; then, as I went to take it, he grabbed it away and instead pushed me out of the door. I'd thought he was calling the police when I was being held up, but he only did it after I hobbled to a pay phone to call them myself.

I'm not sure what I said but I remember screaming over and over at the operator that I'd been robbed. On 911, the call operator lady kept saying she couldn't understand me, so I screamed into the phone that I was Eminem's mom. I believe all they heard was 'Eminem'. I spoke to bystanders who said they'd chased the kid and that police were only a block away. Slowly the police came up the block and pulled in, and suddenly there were helicopters overhead. Over the crackle of radios I heard someone say Eminem had been carjacked, that they had the kid in custody and that the car and the purse were recovered. When they discovered it was me who'd been robbed, not my son, they were dismissive.

They took me off to the nearest police station in Oak Park, sat me down and treated me like I was the criminal. I just sat there in my imitation-poodle coat, clutching Itchy's lead and crying. They asked if I wanted to phone Marshall – I suppose they wanted their own fifteen minutes of fame, too. I shook my head.

It hadn't taken them long to pick up a suspect. The kid was two and a half miles away. He jumped out of my car and was running through someone's backyard when the police grabbed him after bystanders blocked him in. He refused to talk, saying he wanted his mom and lawyer there. My purse, with all my money, identity papers and photos of my kids, was gone.

I was told by police officers that if I calmed down they would bring me my purse. They then took turns coming into and out of the room, but all of a sudden everyone was gone. When I made repeated requests for information, I was ignored by officers who appeared to be at loggerheads with each other. Eventually one officer came in, shut the door behind him and told me there was no purse. I was really upset by now, and felt doubly angry that I wasn't being listened to, and nor was I given my personal possessions back there and then. I was sick of the whole thing. While being driven back to the police department after the incident, in shock and tightly clutching Itchy's leash, all I could say was I couldn't believe how baby-faced the suspect kid looked. The police made a note of my observation.

It didn't take long for the media to hear about the carjacking, either. By the next morning I was making headlines all over the world. My phone rang off the hook with friends and relatives calling to make sure I was OK. The only person who didn't seem to know about it was Marshall. I tried to play that down, telling the local media that he 'apparently must not be in town'.

It was weeks before Marshall acknowledged that anything had happened. I heard him in the background one day when I was on the phone to Nathan, poking fun at me, saying, 'It had to happen on 8 Mile, didn't it?'

I got the impression he didn't believe I'd been attacked. A close friend of mine made a few enquiries. He said my assailant was a crazy guy who'd bragged about robbing Eminem's mom. The kid claimed he didn't realise it was me until he got up close, then he recognised me from the TV. Who's to say what really happened here?

In fairness to Marshall, he did have other things on his mind. In February Kim was sent to jail. She'd failed a urine test and admitted to her probation officer that she'd used cocaine. I can't say I felt much sympathy for her. She never would toe the line, acting as though she could do anything she pleased.

Marshall often joked that if Kim fell into a heap of

manure she'd come up smelling of roses. She served less than a month in jail. Yet still she didn't learn anything. She received another 140 days' jail in July after dropping out of her court-ordered drug-treatment programme.

I'd joined Amnesty International after seeing how my brother Todd was treated in prison. He came out a broken man. But I wanted James Knott, the sixteen-year-old arrested for robbing me, to be punished – for the carjacking as well. I lost a big part of me that night.

I wasn't even sure that the prosecutors had the right guy. I remember my attacker being around five-foot-nine and 150 pounds (that's 68 kilos, or just over 10 and a half stone). Knott was more like five-foot-two and 98 pounds (only around 45 kilos, or 7 stone). But I was told he'd admitted to it.

In April the judge ruled that Knott, who was tried as an adult, had to go to prison for such a serious offence. He pleaded guilty to carjacking and robbery, was sentenced to four years in jail and ordered to pay me $3,573 compensation. Needless to say, he never gave me a penny.

My poor dog Itchy suffered more psychologically than I did. To this day he freaks out if we stop at a gas station. I'm just ultra-careful now. I try to avoid those places if it's late. Itchy landed on me when he was flung from the car and, although I didn't know it then, I broke a bone in my foot. But by May I had more serious health issues.

I'd found a walnut-sized lump in my breast. The doctors believed it was cancerous.

By then I was really struggling financially. I had no health insurance and I had to pay cash upfront for a mammogram. Then I was told to regain my strength before surgery. I'd lost 10 pounds (4.5 kilos). My weight was hovering around 84 pounds (38 kilos, or 6 stone). I reacted by going into denial.

Word obviously got back to Marshall. There had been stories all over his fan sites that I was dying. Out of the blue, he called.

'How are you?' he asked. He sounded genuinely concerned.

'I'm OK, son,' was all I managed. I didn't want to burden him with my problems. I tried to switch the subject to other things, such as Hailie, but he asked me to fax my medical papers to his management company. He offered to pay my health insurance. I told him I didn't want his money but he insisted I send them over.

What I would really have liked was the chance for a face-to-face meeting with Marshall. I wanted to sit down with him and talk the way we used to before he was famous. It wasn't to be, but at least he'd called.

My brother Todd was my rock throughout many of the ordeals I'd been through. As far as I was concerned, he'd saved my life when I was pregnant with Nathan and chased off the mad knifeman Mike Harris, the guy who had attacked me when I was pregnant. He'd also kept me sane during the worst times of my life, making me laugh, always supporting me. Todd was a father figure to my sons, helping both of them whenever they needed it.

Todd was more upset about my breast-cancer diagnosis than I was. He was terrified of losing me. I remember he kept saying, 'You are not leaving me behind.' Time and again I reassured him I was not dying.

Todd's life hadn't been easy, either. From the moment he was born I'd tried to protect him, first from Dad, who claimed he was someone else's child, then from our stepfathers. Todd was big for his age and clumsy, forever falling out of trees and having accidents. Like me, he'd made up for our awful childhood by vowing to become the best father ever. He adored his children, Todd Jr and daughters Christina and Tara, by his first wife Sherry, along with Corey and Bobbie, his sons by his second wife Janice. In the way that I spoiled Marshall and Nathan, smothering them in love, Todd did the same with his children. There was nothing he wouldn't do for them. But, just as Marshall did, his kids rebelled in their teens.

It probably didn't help that he'd spent seven years in jail after killing Janice's brother Mike Harris in self-defence. Todd had never been in trouble with the police before, but Harris had driven him to the brink. As I discussed earlier, Todd had grabbed an antique gun to defend himself, shot Harris and had then gone straight to the nearest police station to hand himself in. He refused to plead temporary insanity – he knew he'd killed in self-defence. But, after a two-week trial, the jury disagreed. He was sentenced to a total of eight years in jail – five for manslaughter and three for gun possession. I was in shock as the verdict was read out. I'd found the trial process very disturbing – in particular I was very unhappy about the choice of witnesses, the evidence heard by the jury and also about the lack of a transcript of Todd's trial.

It was a living hell for my brother. He was moved constantly; each prison was worse than the previous one. There's a certain type of person who picks on bigger people. Todd was picked on constantly by other inmates and the guards. When fights broke out he often got the blame. He was placed in solitary confinement and – on one occasion – a cage. The segregation cells were windowless concrete boxes, barely 6 feet (about a metre) wide. After forty-eight hours in one of those, psychosis sets in.

I did my best to keep Todd's spirits up. The worst year was when Nathan was taken into foster care. I flitted between Missouri and Michigan, trying to see both of them. I spent so long in prison visiting Todd that often I felt as though I were an inmate, too. I could tune into his pain.

I contacted Amnesty International about the prison conditions. I've been an active member ever since. It isn't just the Third World that mistreats its prisoners. America, in my mind, is one of the worst offenders. And the politicians wonder why so many of our prisoners come out of jail worse than before they went in!

When Todd was finally released, after serving almost seven years of his eight-year sentence, he was a broken man. His health was terrible after years of prison abuse and lack of medical treatment, but he vowed to start anew.

His marriage broke up after his release. He moved in with Nan and cared for her until she died in 2000.

He inherited her house. I was so happy she left it to him. It helped him get a foothold. He started his own heating business and threw himself into the music scene. He had a band called Nemesis and wrote all their material. They were beautiful songs.

Todd helped me through some of my worst moments with the press. He defended me time after time. Much was made of Marshall's dysfunctional family – and Todd's imprisonment was used to add street credibility to his hard-man image back in 1999 and 2000. But, just as he did with me, Marshall vented much of his anger on Todd. He accused him of selling stories to the media and his precious belongings on the Internet. Yet, still Todd defended him, telling anyone who would listen that Marshall and I had enjoyed a close, loving relationship until Kim came along.

'A daughter is a daughter for life. A son is a son till he takes a wife,' he told salon.com in a 2000 interview explaining how Marshall and I had become estranged.

Todd fell in love with a woman called Kathy, a friend of my sister Tanya, who introduced them. They were so happy together and he became a father to her two teenage children. But she ran off with one of his band members. Then he met another woman also called Kathy, who had a young son. He aimed to start a new life once again. He finally bought a place up in northern Michigan with five acres of land, and he planned to completely revamp all the wiring, plumbing, flooring and so on to make it a beautiful home.

Because Todd's health suffered so much in jail – he had suffered a severely dislocated shoulder, several broken shoulder bones inside and had serious liver problems – he got into debt paying his bills and was forced to sell Nan's house for $45,000. It had been in the family for fifty years but I understood why he needed to sell it. The buyer promptly put it on eBay for more than a million. Marshall was furious and got madder still when Todd appeared on a DVD about him called *Behind the Mask* and set up an Eminem webpage.

Todd also started to write a book. It was about his life and the horrible things that had happened to him in jail. Interviewed by the local *Macomb Daily* in 2002, Todd admitted his actions hadn't gone down well in the family.

'He's [Marshall] mad. They're all mad at me, everyone in the whole family. But I do what I have to do.'

When Todd first came out of prison and his marriage broke up he was depressed. His poor health didn't help his state of mind. But suicide was not something he even considered. After selling Nan's place, he and Kathy had focused on creating their new home together. He was happier than I'd seen him in years, although he then decided to sell his place up north and travel by motor home across the country.

In September 2004 he was arrested twice. Todd, who

225

rarely touched alcohol, had broken his hip and was awaiting surgery when the police pulled him over. He was asked to stand on one leg – part of the sobriety test that involves checking a person's balance. My brother explained he couldn't do it because of his injury. He was held overnight in the local jail, where his captors played Eminem music loudly over the intercom.

After he was released on bail I took him to hospital, where he underwent surgery to have five screws put in his hip. The doctors had fears that he might have contracted Hepatitis-C, and Todd said he'd been treated like a leper as a result. On the way home his girlfriend Kathy called to say she and her son were trapped in the house by a neighbour's Rottweiler dog. They'd been having problems with the family, so Todd defied the doctors who had told him not to drive and went straight over there.

The dog chased Todd's car, then ran off. The neighbours claimed he ran it over, there was an altercation and the police were called. The following week he was charged with cruelty, torturing and abusing an animal It was all totally untrue – in fact, I found out later that the dog was fine – but if found guilty Todd faced five years in jail.

Todd loved animals and was terribly upset he'd been accused of harming one. I offered to sell my property in Missouri to pay for a decent lawyer and while Todd stayed at my house in Michigan, as a condition of his bail, I set off to sort out the sale.

The 17th of October was Marshall's thirty-second

226

birthday. As always I sent a card, along with a cheque. And as usual I heard nothing back. I arrived in Missouri, after a two-day drive from Michigan, just before midnight, switched off the phone and went to bed. At 1 a.m. I was awoken by my brother-in-law Lynard and nephew Jonathan banging on my door. They were screaming that Todd had been shot.

Todd was back at hospital, in intensive care. The doctors said he would not recover. At 4.40 a.m. the decision was made to take him off life support. Todd died 23 minutes later; he was just forty-two. To date I have never forgiven myself for not taking him along with me when I went to Missouri. Maybe he'd still be alive; I know he would.

In the dark days that followed, I tried to find out what had happened. But everyone, including the police, gave me the runaround. Todd's death was ruled a suicide. He was said to have been depressed about the problems with his neighbour's dog, along with an arrest for allegedly drink-driving, and had shot himself in the face.

I didn't buy that for a second, and nor did his girlfriend Kathy. He'd been in great spirits, calling her at 3.30 p.m. from a friend's house to say he was trying to persuade someone to give him a lift because he didn't have enough gasoline to pick up his son from his ex-wife Janice and return home.

Then, at 12.30 a.m., Junior, as we all call Todd's eldest, phoned 911 to say he'd found his father parked outside his house in New Baltimore. He was in the driver's seat, unconscious. I was told he had shot himself.

227

One of the first of many unanswered questions I asked was what was he doing way down in southern Michigan at his eldest son's house when he hadn't had enough gas to drive to his ex-wife's home earlier on.

There was no suicide note on him, although a piece of paper with the words 'Nate's life' was in his pocket. The detectives seemed to think that was relevant. In fact, it was the password to my computer. Todd had been using my Internet to research his upcoming legal cases. Other so-called notes were in the glove compartment. One note was addressed to 'Mother'. Not only did it not resemble Todd's writing, but he'd never usually addressed her as Mother – it was Maw or Mom.

One of the most upsetting things was the reaction of the local paper. It printed a front page piece dredging up the fact that Todd had killed his brother-in-law Mike Harris. The article was in bad taste and added insult to injury at a time when we were all so upset.

I was in tears when Marshall called me. I hoped he'd know what to do.

But the old anger returned.

'I'll pay for that piece of shit's funeral but don't ask me to attend,' he said.

'Why are you being like this?' I wailed at him.

'He bashed me all over the media,' Marshall said.

'Todd loved you,' I told him.

Marshall ignored that. He just told me to put a cap of $7,000 on the funeral expenses. He had no intention of paying any more.

The funeral home was packed. We had an open casket so people could see him. Then, after a short cremation service, Todd's ashes were placed in an urn at the foot of Ronnie's grave in St Joseph. It was all over so quickly. Kathy returned home to discover the house where they lived had been broken into during the funeral. Among the things stolen was Todd's computer, with his almost-finished book manuscript on it, and lots of Marshall's drawings. The police didn't even bother to investigate. Todd's will was also destroyed. I'd notarized the first one in 2001, and he showed me the one he drew up in 2003. It was never recorded yet he told everyone close to him where to find it if anything ever happened to him. Someone broke into the lock-box it was in, and destroyed it.

The police swept Todd's death under the carpet, too. When I rummaged through the car glove compartment I found a large manila envelope with all his papers and registration within. I phoned my mom, as some of the papers were addressed to her, and she wanted to see them so I made copies, also informing the officers – who threatened to charge me for tampering with evidence if I didn't give it up. When I asked – time after time – why there was no blood on the ceiling of the car they just ignored me. Apparently there were no pictures of this. I had too many questions. I was told the passenger door had to be pryed open yet they claimed it was never opened. I knew better – in the past, Todd had carried passengers who'd used that door to get in and out of that side. There were way too many things wrong.

Todd was six foot tall and 185 pounds (that's 84 kilos, or over 13 stone). He had long legs, yet the driver's seat was pulled forward so he would have been scrunched up over the steering wheel. There was blood on the headrest but none anywhere else. The impact would have sprayed blood everywhere.

Todd had used a gun once – and paid a terrible price for it. After killing Mike Harris he was rightly wary of firearms. He had a criminal record and could not be around them. When Nan died he gave me her antique pistols, since he didn't want them in the house.

To this day it is not clear where the rifle that killed him came from. Todd was said to have got it at a pawnshop on a Sunday night in exchange for his beloved guitar; then he was supposed to have borrowed it from a friend. It was a gun used for shooting animals but was unlikely to kill a human.

According to the police, Todd was found in the driver's seat with the engine still running and all the doors locked. The rear window on the driver's side had been smashed through. Todd was strapped into his seatbelt clutching the rifle, which was underneath his jacket, to his hooded sweatshirt. He was supposed to have fired upwards under his chin. I've had several six-foot-tall, average-built men scrunch into a car with the seat pulled forward to try to recreate that scene. It's not possible. And the gunshot wound was to the back of his head, not his chin.

I have constantly asked the police for a copy of the

911 tape and for pictures of the crime scene. They just give me the runaround. I was sent the wrong 911 recording tape. When I asked for the right one, I was told it had been erased. And they couldn't show me the gun either.

One officer actually asked, 'Who the hell was this guy anyway? He was no one.' Another claimed the opposite, saying Todd's death wasn't going to be investigated because of who he was. I assume it was because he was Marshall's uncle. Then he asked me if I could get signed posters for his kids.

One of the officers had lived near Todd once. He seemed to have a massive downer on the entire family. I found him especially hard to deal with because he was so negative about everything.

December was the hardest: it would have been Todd's forty-third birthday; then there was Christmas. Todd had always loved the holiday season and we usually spent it together. I felt as though I'd lost everything precious in my life.

There were so many unanswered questions. Just a month before he died I'd been at his hospital bedside when he came round after the hip surgery. He said then, 'Sister, I'm so glad to see you. I thought I'd died,' as he squeezed my hand.

If he was so happy to have survived that, why did he kill himself a month later? Also, we were so close. Why didn't he leave a note for me?

His last words to me were: 'Sister, all I want is for

everyone to get along.' He hated the fact that our family was fractured and that Marshall and I were estranged.

My health went to hell in a hand basket: I suffered a small heart attack, I kept losing weight, my entire body seemed to be falling apart. The only good thing that happened was that I discovered I had been misdiagnosed. I didn't have breast cancer after all.

I was trying to investigate Todd's death. There was no way he killed himself. I employed private investigators to help but they got the same runaround as I did. They said my brother had been executed lobotomy style. In other words he did not shoot himself. Todd's then-girlfriend Kathy agrees with me but she has hit the same brick walls as I have. Todd's eldest son, Junior, evicted her shortly after he was made executor of the estate.

Now I have heard rumours about who killed Todd. I've even witnessed a certain someone bragging it was assisted suicide, claiming Todd had begged for help in killing himself.

I pleaded with the office of Macomb County prosecuting attorney, Eric Smith, for help. I handed over all of the medical records, the autopsy report, everything I had. But months went by before I received a short letter saying, 'This office concludes there is no credible evidence to change the findings of the initial investigation and the medical examiner's conclusion, which is suicide.' Something I find very hard to credit is the report of the medical examiner. It seems a prominent scar on Todd's stomach and chest area was completely missed by the examiner even though the same hospital had dealt with the surgery at the time and had logged the details. How could the coroner not notice it?

Now I know most people would give up. But I promised Todd that if anything ever happened to him I would get to the bottom of it. I've spent thousands of dollars on lawyers and private eyes. I'm happy to spend every last penny finding out the truth. My brother had such a hard life here on earth, and I'd like to think God has given him everything now he's in heaven. That's the only thing that keeps me sane.

This book is dedicated to, among others, Todd, along with our younger brother Ronnie. Over the years I have been asked many times to tell my side of the Eminem story but I always refused. Then it struck me that I owed it to Todd to write about what happened to him. If just one person comes forward with information to help me solve what happened, then cleaning out my closet, telling the world about the deeply private things I once hoped to keep secret, will have been worth it. It's been a painful journey but foremost in my mind is that I'm doing it for Todd. I haven't given up on solving his death, and, if there is a lawyer or private detective reading this who would like to help me, please get in touch. I need someone who isn't afraid of asking difficult questions and getting answers – someone with a strong backbone.

Other members of my family tell me to forget it. I know it won't bring my brother back, but I need to know what really happened to him. I need closure.

# CHAPTER TWENTY-FIVE

Marshall gave an interview to *Vanity Fair*, one of the most respected magazines in the world. He expressed regrets about his fame, saying, 'I would take it back to where I made a comfortable living. To where I would just make music, have people appreciate it, even if it's a few people who appreciate it, and be able to walk to a mall, walk to a store.

'When you get fame and fortune and you make something of your life and become successful... a whole new slew of problems that I never expected... come along with it. Sometimes I battle with these demons that make me say in my head, "I'm not going to be locked in a cage, I'm gonna walk in this place and I'm not going to sign autographs."'

It's been said that Sigmund Freud, the father of

psychoanalysis, would have a field day dissecting my son. It's true. Marshall is a mass of contradictions – he's shy, suffers terrible stage fright yet tours constantly and is among the most instantly recognisable people in the world. I believe he'd have been far happier writing lyrics and producing away from the spotlight. Sometimes I wish we hadn't moved back to Michigan in 1987, where he got involved with hardcore rap. If we'd stayed in Missouri he'd have maybe worked on a farm or in a factory. I don't know if that would have made him happier but I do know we would not be estranged.

Lots of therapists have contacted me over the years to offer their opinion on my son's behaviour. One called me from Britain to say that up-and-coming celebrities often claim to have suffered tough childhoods to help their careers. They invent a new persona. In Marshall's case he has become Slim Shady and Eminem. With these celebrities, alcohol and drugs colour their memories, and after a while they honestly think the bad things really happened.

I suppose it's like O J Simpson, who truly believes he did not murder his wife Nicole, or John Mark Karr, who confessed to killing the child beauty queen JonBenet Ramsey when DNA and all other evidence said otherwise. Forensic psychologists say that, if either man took a lie-detector test, they would pass. Simpson believes he's innocent; Karr believed he was guilty.

I'm not the only parent of a celebrity who has seen history rewritten. A dear friend of mine who is a celebrity's father has been through similar issues since his son became famous. Like me, he couldn't get through on the phone to his son. He would try to reach him, but his son's staff would ignore him. He continues to try and break through this barrier of employees, advisers and hangers-on – and I wish him the best, as I know how he feels.

In my heart I know Marshall still loves me, he's just confused. He says now he doesn't even remember 1999, the year he made it big, toured constantly and married Kim for the first time. Everything is just a fuzzy memory.

Yet look at his lyrics: the people he is closest to – Hailie, Kim, Nathan and me – are mentioned constantly.

By 2004 I'd stopped listening to Marshall's songs or watching his videos. They were too upsetting. But in October I heard about the promo for his single 'Mosh'. He was playing George W. Bush reading a children's book upside down to a roomful of kids. My first reaction was to cringe: in America you just don't make fun of the President. But Marshall had never cared about that, so much so that the Secret Service had made enquiries into his anti-Bush remarks the previous year. Now here was my son openly mocking the commander-in-chief's intelligence.

I puffed up with pride when I realised Marshall was using his influence to encourage youngsters to get out and vote in the November elections. I've always been an activist, volunteering at polling stations and putting up placards for local politicians. My brother Todd was the same. Now many Americans, especially the young, don't bother even to *register* to vote, so I was delighted that Marshall was rallying his fans. In Michigan he'd been involved in an earlier voting drive and, even though 'Mosh' was released too late for many to register, and Bush was re-elected, I did read that 20 million people under the age of thirty voted – 4.5 million more than in 2000. I like to think Marshall helped get the word out.

Marshall was arguably the most controversial musician of his generation, but, whereas before he'd been pilloried for inciting hated against women and gays, he had matured into rap's elder statesman. In the beginning he thrived on confrontation, mocking everyone from the Spice Girls and boy bands to MTV presenters and former President Bill Clinton. But he now sought to be the peacemaker. His protégé 50 Cent – whose *Get Rich or Die Tryin'* was the biggest breakthrough album of 2003 – had been involved in numerous spats with New York rapper Ja Rule and his Murder Inc. crew. Marshall got caught up in the feud by default – Ja Rule mocked both Kim and Hailie in song. Marshall answered him, but, instead of being goaded into what could quite easily have spiralled into a new rap war, my son penned 'Like Toy Soldiers', a track that basically said let's stop pretending we're gangsters. Ja Rule agreed to the ceasefire but I was proud that my son had proved to be the bigger man by offering reconciliation.

I'm reminded now of the St Joseph newspaper horoscope for the day Marshall was born on 17 October 1972. Aside from saying he would never turn his artistic talents into commercial worth – clearly wrong – it stated he'd make an excellent jurist or keeper of the peace. I laughed about that when Marshall first became famous, because he caused trouble everywhere. Now finally, at the age of thirty-two, he'd grown up into a typical Libran, weighing up arguments and working out the best way forward.

Regardless of whether I listen to Marshall's music more than once, I still buy his CDs to support him. His winter 2004 album *Encore* was another big hit, selling a respectable 9 million copies worldwide. He was also working with a stable of new artists as well as his old mates Proof and D-12. But speculation was rife that he intended to retire.

Just like David Bowie, who thirty years earlier killed off his alter ego Ziggy Stardust at London's Hammersmith Odeon by announcing it was the last show he'd ever do, Marshall seemed to be signalling the end of Eminem. He'd scattered clues throughout *Encore*, which ended with his gunning down the audience before shooting himself. I couldn't bring myself to look at the cover, which pictured him with a gun in his mouth and a suicide note.

He was certainly exhausted. The last thing he wanted was to go on tour again. Marshall seemed happy only when holed up in his mansion with Hailie and her cousin Lainie playing happy families. There he enjoys doing all the daddy things with them, such as shooting basketball hoops on the driveway and helping them decorate the house at Christmas, Easter and Hallowe'en.

I have no doubt that he loves Hailie more than anyone in the world. He's certainly stricter with her than I ever was with him. He also keeps a fatherly eye on Nathan. They all have chores and have to work for their pocket money.

He finally saw the light and got rid of my half-sister Betti and her husband Jack. But he replaced them with an army of hangers-on and record-company loafers. Whatever has happened between Marshall and me, I'm still his mother and I worry about him every single day. I have my own people; sometimes they phone begging me to intervene because they're concerned about Marshall.

I worry about his health all the time. He's always had high blood pressure and his cholesterol levels must be sky high. He tells fans that Taco Bell – the Mexican burrito chain – is his favourite fast food. In reality, he orders filet-mignon takeout from an expensive restaurant almost every evening. I dread to think what his bills are – he pays for everyone hanging around the house.

It's said that Marshall's a multimillionaire but the record business is dying. He's suffered financially because everyone downloads, shares files and copies. I'm told *8 Mile* made $215 million, of which Marshall got very little. He has several accountants handling his finances. He's creative. He doesn't have to balance his chequebook or do many other things like that.

By the summer of 2005 Marshall was exhausted and rumours of his retirement reached fever pitch when

Proof told the *Detroit Free Press*, 'Em has definitely gotten to the level where he feels he's accomplished everything he can accomplish in rap. He wants to kick back and get into producing things.'

Marshall vehemently denied that, telling MTV, 'When I say I'm taking a break, I'm taking a break from my music to go into the studio and produce my other artists. When I know my next move, I'll tell everyone my next move.'

But it didn't matter what Marshall wanted to do – his management team insisted he branch out still further. He inked a deal with Sirius satellite radio for his own twenty-four-hours-a-day music channel.

Marshall seems to have energy to spare. He's a perfectionist, more than happy to work eighteen hours without a break to get something right. Instead of kicking back and enjoying time off, he seemed to be working harder than ever. He'd always been an insomniac but his sleeping habits were getting more bizarre. He often goes to bed early, nods off for a few hours, then writes through the night. He never takes vacations, travelling for work, rarely for pleasure.

The Anger Management Tour had been on the road for three years. The hip-hop extravaganza featured Marshall and an ever-changing stable of acts. The third instalment, with 50 Cent, Obie Trice, Lil Jon, Proof, D-12, Stat Quo and The Alchemist, was punishing.

Starting on 7 July in Indianapolis, Indiana, they were crisscrossing the country doing twenty-two shows, culminating in Detroit on 12 August. Then there were ten European concerts, beginning in Hamburg on 1 September, ending seventeen days later in Dublin.

The tour bus crashed, sparking a seven-vehicle pile-up, just outside Kansas City. Marshall wasn't on board but others, including The Alchemist, were badly injured. There were constant grumbles – everyone was sick and tired of touring.

Britain's tabloid newspapers, forever spoiling for a fight with Marshall, suggested he'd become a diva. It was reported his backstage demands for the Manchester concert included three bottles of Cristal champagne, two bottles of Hennessy cognac, two cases of Heineken beer, a twenty-four-piece bucket of Kentucky Fried Chicken, plus an assortment of sweets and chocolate.

It didn't sound like the healthiest of diets. But, in the event, it didn't matter. Days after the American leg had ended, the European tour was abruptly cancelled.

Marshall's record company issued a terse statement, simply saying, 'Eminem is currently being treated for exhaustion, complicated by other medical issues. The shows are not expected to be rescheduled.'

It didn't take the media long to find out the real reason. Marshall had checked into rehab for sleeping-pill abuse. According to the *Irish Daily Star*, he was addicted to Stilnoct, a super-strength, short-term medication.

Slane Castle just outside Dublin was to have been the biggest concert of the tour: some 80,000 tickets had sold out in just two hours. The castle owner, Lord

Mountcharles, was furious, saying Marshall would never be welcome back there.

'I don't think the Rolling Stones or U2 would cancel a section owing to nervous exhaustion. I don't deem that I've had a proper explanation,' he said.

I couldn't believe it. My son was in hospital and some aristocrat was moaning he'd have to make refunds. As always when it comes to my son, the concert promoters threatened legal action.

As Marshall recovered in hospital, two new lawsuits emerged. A truck driver and his wife, who claimed they'd been injured in the tour-bus pile-up, announced they were seeking unspecified damages. Then my half-sister Betti and her husband Jack jumped into the fray. They wanted $350,000 cash and ownership of a house Marshall had had built when they worked for him. They claimed he was trying to evict them from the property and had reneged on a promise to pay them $100,000 a year.

I tried desperately to reach out to Marshall, through his bodyguards and his Shady Records staff. But no one would tell me where he was. I was pretty sure he'd checked into the Brighton Hospital, Michigan's largest chemical-dependency treatment centre. But no one there could give me any answers, citing patient confidentiality. As I understand it, he'd checked in there briefly a year or so earlier. One woman I spoke to was really sweet, saying that, if he was there, I could go to family therapy sessions, that it would help him. Unfortunately, her hands were tied because he – technically – wasn't there.

I did discover, though, that Kim was back on the scene. I worried that she'd lead him astray again.

The music critics, along with the BBC, CNN and other respected international news agencies such as Reuters and the Associated Press, leaped on Marshall's problems. While noting he was a nine-times Grammy winner, a one-man industry who had generated record sales of $1 billion and made rap mainstream, they seemed to think his career was over.

He confounded them by releasing a greatest-hits album, *Curtain Call*, which was Marshall's fourth straight Number 1 album. After just two days on sale it entered the British charts at Number 1 and remained there for five weeks throughout the all-important Christmas period. The single 'When I'm Gone', one of three new tracks, seemed to indicate he was retiring. In reality it was another love song to Hailie. Just as he had in '97 Bonnie and Clyde' and 'Mockingbird', he makes clear that Hailie is the centre of his universe. It begins with Hailie accusing him of loving his fame and fortune more than his family. As she leaves he takes a gun, shouts, 'Die, Shady!' and then kills his alter ego before waking up to realise he's just had a bad dream.

The album sold 6 million copies worldwide. Not bad for a greatest-hits album by someone trying desperately to take a break.

# CHAPTER TWENTY-SIX

Marshall's remarriage to Kim was the worst-kept secret in the world. Considering they'd managed to keep the first, seven years earlier at the start of his meteoric career, under wraps always amazed me. We were naïve in those days, yet not a word leaked out from his family, the church or the staff at St Joseph City Hall who'd stayed open late especially to issue the marriage licence to their hometown superstar. Yet, the second time around, when he had an army of people to protect him, the details flooded out.

A member of Kim's family sold a wedding invitation to America's *Star* magazine. They splashed it across a page, giving the date and Marshall's words on the invitation: 'This day I will marry my best friend, the one I laugh with, live for, love.'

Once again a stream of reporters phoned me. They wanted to know why I wasn't attending.

Kim had obviously fallen out with her twin sister Dawn, since she wasn't on the guest list, either. But Kim's mother and stepfather, who hadn't been invited the first time around, were. Marshall was now rap royalty and the VIP guests included 50 Cent, Obie Trice, G-unit and D-12.

Proof was best man, albeit a reluctant one. Like me, he'd seen the havoc Kim created and tried to persuade Marshall against tying the knot again. Proof was one of the few people Marshall listened to. They'd known each other since they were teenagers, struggling to get noticed on the Detroit hip-hop scene.

But Marshall insisted he knew what he was doing. Among other things, ten-year-old Hailie wanted her parents to be together. She was finally going to be a flower girl and Marshall refused to disappoint her.

Kim wanted a big white wedding to impress her family and friends. Even when they were poor, Marshall had promised she'd get one eventually. Now he was in a position to give her that dream. It's weird, but even after all his incredible achievements, he was still trying to please Kim and prove himself worthy of her. He truly loved her and I think he always hoped she felt the same.

I learned of the wedding through friends and smiled when I read that Kim – who I'm told hadn't bothered with underwear at her first wedding – had indeed worn a traditional white gown. Marshall arrived at the ceremony in a crisp black suit to the sound of his own music. Luis Resto, one of his songwriting team, played 'Mockingbird' on the piano as he walked into Meadow Brook Hall in Rochester Hills.

The 1,200-acre estate was once the home of Matilda Dodge Wilson, widow of the motor pioneer John Dodge. Designed to look like an English Tudor manor, it has 110 rooms and is one of the most popular wedding venues for Michigan's affluent elite. Marshall's first wedding was a hastily scrambled affair at St Joseph's South Park Church followed by a few drinks at a local bar. This time, the eighty-five guests dined on steak and lobster washed down with fine champagne.

I tried not to read the newspaper stories but I gave in eventually, letting a friend read the *Detroit Free Press*'s account of the celebrations to me. Reporter Brian McCollum described it as a 'quietly dignified occasion', quoting an anonymous guest saying it was 'a real classy, intimate affair'. Another added, 'It was one of the most peaceful weddings I've ever been to. This is exactly what Marshall has been looking for.'

As always with Kim, the peace didn't last long. In April 2006 – eighty-two days after the wedding – Marshall filed for divorce. My heart went out to him.

So what went wrong? The things that always went wrong with Marshall and Kim: they can't live with each other; they can't live without each other; she thrives on drama, he likes peace and quiet; she claimed he was still taking drugs, he denied it.

From what I can gather, Kim took off at the beginning of March. She always disappeared when she didn't get her own way. Marshall couldn't find her anywhere and he conceded that the reunion had been a humiliating – and costly – mistake.

'There has been a breakdown in the marriage relationship to the extent that the objects of matrimony have been destroyed and there remains no reasonable likelihood that the marriage can be preserved,' his divorce papers read.

Kim's lawyer, Michael J. Smith, who had been a guest at the wedding and instrumental in sorting out the prenup, responded, 'It comes to us as somewhat of a surprise. But we have to deal with it.'

Naturally, Kim announced she was seeking a financial settlement. I had to wonder just how much money she could possibly need.

Interviewed on Detroit's Mojo Radio, she claimed Marshall was 'not himself', refused to go to counselling and was still taking drugs.

Marshall, listening at home, emailed the radio station to say, 'Her allegations regarding my status post-rehab are both untrue and unfortunate.'

I tried to reach out to Marshall, leaving messages for him because I wanted him to know I was there. Whatever my feelings for Kim, it breaks my heart when my son is upset.

A few days later, on 11 April, my phone started ringing off the hook again. Reporters from all over the world left messages. I ignored the calls, letting my voicemail pick up. Then Nathan called me, crying hysterically. He was screaming that Proof had been shot. Proof was dead.

I'd known Proof since he was just DeShaun Holton, another teenager rapping alongside Marshall in the basement. He'd always been such a lovely young man. He and Marshall were always together. It was Proof who encouraged my son to get on stage and trade insults at the Hip-Hop Shop. He calmed his stage fright and – like me – told Marshall that he could achieve anything he wanted.

With other pals, they called themselves the Dirty Dozen. That group became D-12 – and they'd made a pact that whoever became famous first would take the others along for the ride. Marshall had kept that promise, producing a string of hits for D-12 and encouraging Proof to release his own solo album *Searching for Jerry Garcia*.

Like Marshall, Proof had, in 1999, featured in *The Source* magazine's 'Unsigned Hype' column. When Marshall's career took off, Proof toured with him and provided a shoulder for him to lean on. He was one of the few people my son trusted because they'd been together for so long.

Marshall was spotted leaving his mansion in tears. He'd lost his oldest friend and the one person he listened to, who always told him the truth. Proof pulled him up on his suspected drug taking, his drinking and his fights with Kim. I simply did not want to believe he was dead. I did go and pay my respects to my little friend. I still had a hard time believing it. I could only pray to God to give my sons strength as my heart broke for his family.

It emerged that Proof, who at thirty-two was almost exactly a year younger than Marshall, had got into some sort of altercation over a game of pool at the CCC club, an after-hours bar on the seedy side of 8 Mile. Proof and an Iraq war veteran, Keith Bender, started fighting. Proof apparently hit Bender with his gun, then shot him in the face. Well, that's what the reports say, but I'm not sure anyone knows what really happened. Bender's cousin Mario Etheridge, a bouncer at the club, allegedly fired several warning shots in the air before blasting Proof three times in the head and chest. Proof was pronounced dead on arrival at hospital. Bender, who was thirty-eight, died of his injuries eight days later. Etheridge, who was twenty-eight, was charged with carrying a concealed weapon and discharging a firearm. His legal team successfully argued that he had shot Proof to stop him killing his cousin. I still don't believe it happened this way. Proof was such a kind soul, he would never harm anyone.

Marshall was a pallbearer at Proof's funeral and made one of the most moving tributes I have ever heard. It came straight from the heart.

'You don't know where to begin when you lose somebody who's been such a big part of your life for so long,' he said. 'Proof and I were brothers. He pushed me to become who I am. Without Proof's guidance and encouragement there would have been a Marshall

Mathers, but probably not an Eminem and certainly never a Slim Shady. Not a day will go by without his spirit and influence around us all. He will be missed as a friend, a father and both the heart and ambassador of Detroit hip-hop.

'Right now, there's a lot of people focusing on the way he died. I want to remember the way he lived. Proof was funny, he was smart, he was charming. He inspired everyone around him. He can never, ever be replaced. He was, and always will be, my best friend.'

Fans created a shrine to Proof outside the club. Alongside the balloons, flowers and cuddly toys someone left a packet of Proof's favourite Newport Lights cigarettes and a bottle of Olde English malt whisky.

I worried constantly about gang reprisals. The East Coast–West Coast rap wars killed 2Pac Shakur and the Notorious B.I.G. in the late 1990s. Who was to say the feuding would not start again? Marshall was forever linked with Dr Dre, who'd originally co-founded Death Row Records in Los Angeles with Marion 'Suge' Knight. He'd also dissed his New York rivals in song and in print. And the Detroit hip-hop scene was a hotbed of factions. Proof was always cautious. He had a full-time bodyguard, but that night he was alone in a rough club at 4.30 a.m.

My nerves were hardly calmed when I learned Marshall was getting into road-rage spats with complete strangers. He took his anger over Proof's death out on other drivers at traffic lights or by cutting them off on the freeways. He got into screaming matches for no reason. Aside from the obvious – that he'd be recognised and inevitably sued – I was terrified someone would pull a gun on him.

Now a mother knows when her son is in trouble. One night in August my maternal instincts got the better of me. I drove to Marshall's mansion in the hope of seeing him. As I got out of the car I was shaking but I knew that if we could sit down, just the two of us, for a proper chat we could resolve our issues.

I was stopped by guards before I even reached the front door. They had instructions to let no one in. I broke down in tears as I tried to explain I was his mother.

'He's not here,' one said. 'He's at a dance recital.'

I said I'd wait but a security guard I'd known for some years caught my eye. He knew my brother Todd. He motioned to me as I walked back to my car.

Between sobs I asked him if he knew what had really happened to Todd. He said he knew he hadn't committed suicide.

'Your brother's death was swept under the carpet,' he said. 'Now if you quote me I'll deny saying this. But one day the truth will come out.'

Throughout the last half of 2006 I received several calls from people who care about my son. They all said Marshall was extremely depressed and they were concerned that he could be drinking too much again. As a mother I cannot imagine burying my own child. I can only think of Marshall as the boy he once was – a loving, kind son who grew up to be a massively talented writer and musician.

I fear for him every waking moment. He's become just like Elvis Presley, the star he is constantly compared to for taking the music of black people and turning it mainstream. Elvis retreated behind the gates of his Graceland mansion, surrounded by a Memphis mafia of gun-toting hangers-on, and became a bloated, drugged-up caricature of himself.

I don't want to believe this but I've heard Marshall is doing exactly the same. He's hiding behind the closed doors of his home. I blame Marshall's 'people', an entourage that is supposed to *work* for him, not control him. He's like a puppet around them; he does everything they tell him. Yet they are interested only in the money he makes. There is no one left he can totally trust. Nathan tries to be there for him but Marshall still plays the overprotective big brother.

They get into arguments like normal brothers but it's much harder for my boys because there's always someone on Marshall's payroll playing politics, currying favours and causing trouble between them.

As a mother, of course, I worry. But I do truly believe that Marshall will be back. I'm sure he's biding his time, waiting for the right moment, and when he does return he will be bigger and stronger and more successful than ever. I know my son and he just doesn't give up that easily.

Marshall's divorce battle with Kim continued throughout 2006. It didn't matter that their second union lasted less than three months or that they'd signed a prenup. They couldn't agree on anything and at one stage there was a very real threat that they'd end up going to trial.

The judge appointed a lawyer to mediate, and finally, on 19 December, they reached an out-of-court settlement over property and shared custody. The Michigan media noted that their second divorce was subdued and dignified compared with the mud slinging during the first.

Marshall, who was back at the top of the pop charts with the hip-hop artist and songwriter Akon and their Grammy-nominated collaboration 'Smack That', said not a word as he left the Macomb County Circuit Court.

He'd testily ended 2006 – probably the worst year of his life – by explaining for the hundredth time that he was not retiring, that he'd spent the past twelve months in the studio producing for his stable of protégés. The result was *Eminem Presents: The Re-up*, featuring 50 Cent along with newcomers Bobby Creekwater, Stat Quo and Ca$his. It debuted at Number 2 on the *Billboard* chart in the second week of December to mixed reviews. Marshall appeared on seven tracks and was highly praised. But the critics were clearly expecting more. In Britain, the *Independent* called it 'another water-treading exercise' with 'just a sprinkling of new Eminem originals'. Other critics commented on the gunfire that blasts throughout the second track, 'We're Back', and demanded to know if this was some kind of bizarre tribute to Proof, who appears posthumously on one verse.

Marshall responded, '*The Re-up* is about these new artists and songs. Those unreleased songs with Proof are coming. It isn't fair to them or to the memory of Proof to mix them up.'

As his *annus horribilis* – as Queen Elizabeth II described 1992, when three of her children's marriages broke up and her beloved Windsor Castle burned down – came to an end, Marshall was spinning discs on his Sirius radio station and promising new material galore.

He's signed up to play the bounty hunter Paladin in a big-screen, modern version of the 1950s TV series *Have Gun – Will Travel*, and is working on the soundtrack. Then he's producing the next D-12 album, featuring previously recorded Proof tracks.

As his mother, I just wish he'd sit back and enjoy what he already has. He has fame – and money – beyond his wildest dreams, but it hasn't made him happy. I worry he has forgotten the truly good times we had together. He started out saying his lyrics were a joke and that I wasn't to take them seriously. I played along with that until he started to believe his own hype. We were not estranged until long after that unfortunate Fred Gibson lawsuit. I never intended to take his money, but I did want him to stop maligning me and I felt a retraction letter might help. Yet things got out of control. He's hurt me so much but I'm his mom – I'll forgive him anything.

When Marshall was growing up I tried to protect him

from the world. People warned me then not to shelter him from reality, but I couldn't help it. He was my world. I gave him everything he wanted because I wanted him to be happy. I did the same with Nathan.

As a parent, maybe I should have been a strict disciplinarian. Maybe I should have spanked him, made him do chores and taught him the value of money. He was terribly spoiled and I have no one else to blame for that but myself. I was overprotective.

Yet if I had my time again I would do most of it the same. Our house was always full of his friends. I looked out for them too, helped with whatever they needed, prepared them nice big meals especially at Easter, Thanksgiving and Christmas, and made sure they went to school. We all had so much fun and so many laughs. I did it because I watched my brothers struggle growing up. I always had a soft spot for kids as well as older people. I mothered everyone, and I loved taking my grand-daughter out for pizza.

My biggest regret is taking Kim in. In the beginning I thought everything would be wonderful. She was the daughter I'd always wanted. I had so many plans and dreams and hopes for her. I figured we would be one big happy family. But it wasn't to be. In my opinion, Kim destroyed everything and I wish to God I'd never let her through my front door. That girl destroyed Marshall. If she had been nice it would have been different. MTV once said that he'd destroyed the two women who loved him most – that's Kim and me. But as far as I'm concerned Kim destroyed Marshall and me.

I would love Marshall to fall in love with a really nice girl, someone who loves him for being just him. But, as he revealed in *Vanity Fair*, he no longer knows whom to trust. 'Do they truly love me for me?' he asked. 'The reason they're approaching me is because I'm Eminem. And I will never be able to get over that insecurity... Does this person care about me for me or is too late in the game now? Because I have money, I have fame and I'm who I am.'

When the interviewer suggested he date a fellow celebrity, who would understand his problems, he said, 'Tried that, that didn't work. I've dated a few famous women and gone that route thinking that would work, and they ended up being crazier than I am.'

My poor son just can't win. It's the same with Nathan. He never knows if a girl wants him just to get close to Marshall. Making new friends, of either sex, is hard for both of them. Everyone wants a piece of the Eminem phenomenon. All Nathan wants is to be his own person.

Nathan and I recently had a long chat about our lives. 'I love you and can't think of a better Mom than you,' he said. I said I'm not perfect, nor do I pretend to be, but one thing I'm not, nor have I ever been, is abusive to anyone.

Nathan and many close friends of mine remember things that I have chosen to forget, telling me I haven't been the same since Todd died, that I've had so many struggles in my life, more than my fair share. I hope that in reading my story, people will have a better understanding of my life and the many trials and

257

tribulations I've been through – but I'd like to think I'm a true survivor.

Nathan and I are close and I hope that one day soon Marshall and I can forget our differences and put all this behind us, and once again enjoy the close bond we had in his early years. I have a recurring dream that I am sitting in a restaurant booth when Marshall walks in alone. I catch his eye, I walk over to him and reach out to hug him. The dream usually ends there but it is so vivid that I think about it for hours afterwards. Marshall's not a huggy person any more. He was many years ago but somewhere down the line Kim took that too. Until he was fifteen and she came into our lives he was a loving, sensitive person. Even if he just shook hands with someone, he leaned in for a hug. I think if we sat down together, be it in a restaurant or elsewhere, we might get that back. This may be a dream, but I know that dreams do come true.

So many years have passed since we really talked. I'm sure it's been as hard on him as it has on me. We've lost a lot of time but I believe our love for each other still runs deep. Neither of us cut the umbilical cord.

I hope that if Marshall should read this book he will have a better understanding and realise that the last thing I would ever do is hurt him. I love him too much for that. I have tried to conceal my hurt and pain, but I want him to know, I do love him – always have, always will.

It's said that time heals all wounds, reminding me of a plaque I bought my dear Nan one time. It went like this:

'The Clock of Life is wound but once and no man has the power, to tell just when the hands will stop at late or early hour. Now is the only time we own, so live, love and toil with a will, place no faith in tomorrow for the hands may soon be still... We were born crying; we must learn to laugh.' So true.

I want Marshall to know that I don't blame him for the way things worked out. If he needs me, I'll be there in a heartbeat.